Audio Access Included

SAXOPHONE AEROBICS

BY WOODY MANKOWSKI

T0066605

Contents

To access audio visit:
www.halleonard.com/mylibrary

Enter Code
2484-6078-6109-4122

Cover Illustration by Birck Cox

ISBN 978-1-4950-1462-8

HAL•LEONARD®
CORPORATION

7777 W. BLUEMOUND RD. P.O. BOX 13819 MILWAUKEE, WI 53213

In Australia Contact:
Hal Leonard Australia Pty. Ltd.
4 Lentara Court
Cheltenham, Victoria, 3192 Australia
Email: ausadmin@halleonard.com.au

Visit Hal Leonard Online at
www.halleonard.com

INTRODUCTION

Before I started writing *Saxophone Aerobics*, inventing 365 different workouts seemed like a daunting task. How could I come up with a saxophone book that hadn't been done before? It didn't happen overnight, but it turned out that the exercises were composed with little effort, and that I was able to review and organize much of what I've learned about saxophone and jazz theory. Although it's true that "there is nothing new under the sun," I'm certain no book like this exists for saxophone. It's a daily workout book, combining elements from method and jazz theory books. These exercises are cataloged in such a way that in one year, if all instructions are followed, a saxophonist's sound, technique, and musical consciousness will be greatly improved. Learning everything you can about saxophone technique and sound comes with a caveat: Doubling on both flute and clarinet (at least) is a necessity and a reality for most saxophonists. There are books that deal with doubling, but this book is for saxophone only.

THE WORKOUTS

Whether you purchased this book because you aspire to become a better saxophonist, or the best saxophonist, it will help you achieve that goal. For the most part, *Saxophone Aerobics* will appeal more to advanced saxophone students. My teaching experience is at the college level, but I made sure to start from a point of view that would not scare off beginners. There are plenty of good instruction books available for young players, so I wanted to get to the heavier material as soon as possible.

The difficulty of the exercises progresses in succession, so don't make the mistake of starting at the middle of the book and skipping the beginning part, because you'll be ignoring some critical techniques and theory.

Toward the end of the book, I included information I had never considered before; it is indeed advanced, even for professionals. Most of the recordings you'll hear on the audio tracks went down easily, but some took multiple takes to complete. In those cases, I required a near-perfect example of a technique for which perfection is inappropriate, if not impossible. For example, some of the partials of the overtone series and false fingerings will never be perfectly in tune; they're not supposed to be. It's not a complete waste of your time to try and tune these clumsy notes, but if you choose to save honing them for the future, it probably isn't a bad idea.

It doesn't matter what level you're at; if you start at the beginning of the book, follow all instructions, and learn one exercise per day, you will undoubtedly improve your musical abilities in ways that everyone will notice.

THE TECHNIQUES

There are many techniques unique to the saxophone. I chose those that seemed most necessary. The workouts become increasingly difficult throughout the book. The more technically challenging ones are reserved until after some of the easier ones have been addressed.

The concept of back-tonguing (tonguing on the offbeat) is crucial for any saxophone player to ascertain. It is a constant in most types of music interpretation, and it's expected that you know how to use this type of phrasing in many professional situations: jazz gigs, rock gigs, pops concerts, Broadway pit bands, et al. Much of this book is devoted to the understanding of correct phrasing usage in popular music interpretation, in addition to recognizing odd phrasing combinations in written music.

The overtone series and false fingerings will be covered, not completely, but enough for you to start incorporating their usage. After completing *Saxophone Aerobics*, you can fill a manuscript notebook with your own personal exercises to practice.

Whenever necessary, fingerings have been provided. Most of these fingerings are standard, but some, especially in the altissimo range, are fingerings I use that may not be ideal for every setup. They will work on most saxophones, but you can find other fingerings that might sound better or speak more easily. The ones I use were chosen based on facility and sound quality on my own instruments.

THE THEORY

Saxophone Aerobics includes some basic tools for improvisation, in addition to more advanced theory concepts. We'll briefly study each mode of the major and melodic minor scales, diminished and whole tone scales, bebop and pentatonic scales. Licks, scales, and patterns will appear successively in order of their frequency of use and comprehensibility.

At the end of every week (Sunday), there is a rhythm exercise. Most are melodic, but some will sound and feel foreign. The Sunday workouts are designed to familiarize you with as many rhythms as possible in preparation for sight-reading.

There is a lot of information in this book, and there will be much more to learn on your own. The scales and modes provided will work over corresponding chord symbols, but there's plenty you must do with the rest of your practice time in order to find your own voice. I can't overstress the importance of listening. My best students have always been great listeners. I'm not talking about taking my advice (although that's *nice*); it's more important that they listen to the masters of our art form. Just like any other language, music styles must be heard if they are to be interpreted correctly.

So many of today's technically adept saxophonists sound the same to me, and it's because they play with more brains than heart. Learn everything you can about the saxophone and jazz theory, and when you get an opportunity to improvise in front of an audience, forget it all and just play melody.

HOW TO PRACTICE

If you're serious about becoming a great saxophonist, you should be practicing every day. For advanced saxophonists, the first few weeks of this book might be review. If you're an advanced player, keep yourself interested during the early section of the book by learning the easier exercises in all 12 keys, when appropriate. If you're disciplined enough, learn one exercise per day in all keys, if possible. (For some workouts, it will not be possible/necessary to do this, of course.) It's up to you to challenge yourself to become a better player.

Master each exercise, and then repeat it two to four times. Don't get emotional! Spend as much time as you need to learn an exercise. If it's too hard, postpone it until you're ready to reattempt it. Take as many breaks as you need, drink water, breathe. When you feel like you're not making music anymore, you should stop.

Tips on how to practice the etudes

- Learn one exercise per day. If you miss a day or two because of illness or whatever, pick up where you left off when you recover. You'll probably miss several days over a year. Don't sweat it. This isn't a calendar.

- Use a metronome and set it as slowly as necessary to start. After you've sped up the metronome and can play the exercise at the indicated tempo, you can play it along with the corresponding drum track. Don't tap your foot; this could become a hard habit to break.

- Pay particular attention to the phrasing (slurs, articulations, inflections, dynamics, rests) and play the phrase markings as written. Phrasing is as important as the melody; it's what gives a melody its "personality." The only purpose of many of these etudes is to provide different phrasing combinations for you to practice, so it would behoove you not to ignore any of them.

- Take advantage of all listening suggestions, and check out every saxophonist mentioned by name. Sometimes techniques that are hard to explain are easy to hear and emulate. There is much to be learned from the masters that hasn't been written down, but can be instantly understood with a quick listen. If your goal is to become a professional saxophonist, you should be listening constructively to music that inspires you – for several hours a day, or as much time as you can possibly spare.

- Avoid "flying fingers." Practice in front of a mirror to see how high you lift your fingers off the keys. If they're sticking out and away from the horn when you play, this will hinder your ability to play fast runs. You should be touching the pearls of the keys at all times.

- Don't practice making mistakes. Take it slow, get it right, and move on.

- Use vibrato sparingly. You don't want it to become a habit.

- Be aware of everything you do during practice time.

Practice tips for over-achievers only
- Learn one exercise per day. Yup, even the easy ones (see below).

- Practice the melodic etudes (licks and patterns) with a metronome set at half speed on beats 2 and 4, or set it at one beat per measure, on a beat or offbeat other than 1.

- Whenever possible or worthwhile, practice the lick and pattern etudes in *all 12 keys*, either chromatically or in the Cycle of 4ths (not the Cycle of 5ths: the ii–V–I pattern is built on the interval of a perfect 4th. As improvisers, the perfect 4th is a much more useful interval to be stuck in our head.).

- If possible, play the easier melodic etudes and patterns up an octave. If you are familiar with the altissimo range of the saxophone, go ahead and use it.

- Okay, if you're still bored, learn the next day's workout, but you've still got all the rest of your practicing to do, so think twice.

Happy Practicing!

The licks and patterns in this book are yours to use as you see fit. In improvisation, a *lick* is a series of short digital patterns that have been connected by intervals to create an improvised melody. Digital patterns (1-3-5-7 arpeggios, etc.) belong to the public domain, in the same way that math equations belong to the public domain. There are infinite music patterns within the confines of Western harmony to be discovered on your own. Use the patterns and melodic ideas in *Saxophone Aerobics* to help you come up with your own signature licks.

The difference between weak and strong players is equal to the difference in the time they spend practicing and listening. There is such a thing as natural ability, but determination is the factor that separates the amateurs from the professionals. Knowing what works, and what doesn't, comes from listening. Anyone who sounds like they know what they're doing on their instrument wasn't born that way, they've learned. They are music fanatics. To be a great musician, you have to really, really want it. The more time you spend practicing and listening, the better you will be. It's as simple as that.

As someone who exercises physically on a regular basis, I can attest that the hardest part about working out is getting started. The same is true with practicing your instrument; you have to show up. You already did the easy part… These workouts aren't going to practice themselves.

ABOUT THE ONLINE AUDIO

On the title page of this book you will find a code that allows you to access the online demo tracks. You can listen to these online or download them. There are 52 tracks, one for each week of the year. Within each track, prior to the demonstration, the day's name is spoken (e.g., "Monday"), then the metronome clicks one measure. The demo for Day 365 is at the end of Track 52.

MON

Workout #1   **Drum Tracks:** 22, 23   **Type:** Lick/Pattern   **Genre:** Bossa Nova

Our first workout is a C major scale with gradually larger intervals. Legato tongue each note (da-da-da, not ta-ta-ta).

TUE

Workout #2   **Drum Tracks:** 4–6   **Type:** Pattern   **Genre:** Swing

The first half of this exercise is a pattern using triads dipping down to lead tones in groups of three in the key of F. The second half is a pattern using major triad inversions approached diatonically from a step above. The *bis* key should be used for the B♭ in measure 4. The B♭ bis key is the small key just below the B key in your left hand. Play a B and roll your finger to hold down both the B and the bis keys to sound a B♭. Observe all phrasing and legato markings.

Note: The bis key is sometimes a preferred fingering for middle and high B♭, but use all of them. There are three different fingerings for B♭, and in most cases, the correct fingering won't be given. (It's subjective anyway.) When fingerings aren't indicated, choose the one that best facilitates key movement, and eventually, through practice, the choice will become second nature.

A#/B♭ Bis Key

WED

Workout #3   **Drum Tracks:** 1-3   **Type:** Pattern   **Genre:** Swing

These are G major triads with lead tones. Observe the back-tonguing technique in the phrasing. This phrasing technique will occur throughout this book and is used as the default articulation by most jazz saxophonists to create a hard-swinging style.

THU

Workout #4 **Drum Tracks:** 4–5 **Type:** Lick **Genre:** Swing

The first half of this exercise requires you to slur gradually smaller diatonic intervals of the C major scale. The second half is a swing-era lick. As always, pay attention to all phrase markings.

FRI

Workout #5 **Drum Tracks:** 5–6 **Type:** Scale/Lick **Genre:** Swing

The first half of this exercise is a D major scale workout, the second half is a bebop lick.

SAT

Workout #6 **Drum Tracks:** 1, 2, 4, 5 **Type:** Lick/Pattern **Genre:** Swing

This pattern is based on the up-down alternating 3rds of the F major scale.

SUN

Workout #7 **Drum Tracks:** 22–24, 29, 30 **Type:** Pattern **Genre:** Latin

We will end each week with a rhythm workout. This Latin pattern is similar to something you might see while reading the music of Mongo Santamaria. It incorporates staccato rhythms often used in Afro-Cuban music. The faster you can play this, the better.

WEEK 2

MON

Workout #8   **Drum Tracks:** 13–15   **Type:** Rhythm   **Genre:** Rock

This A minor (C pentatonic) rhythm exercise with typical funk phrasing.

♩ = 96-144

TUE

Workout #9   **Drum Tracks:** 19–21   **Type:** Pattern/Rhythm   **Genre:** Jazz Waltz

This is a fairly easy diatonic ascending pattern in F major. Pay attention to the slur markings.

♩ = 108-152

WED

Workout #10   **Drum Tracks:** 7–9   **Type:** Lick   **Genre:** Shuffle

Play this exercise in G major as smoothly as possible, using legato tonguing (da-da, not ta-ta).

♩ = 92-144

THU

Workout #11 **Drum Tracks:** 22 **Type:** Pattern **Genre:** Jazz Waltz

Here are some rhythms you will encounter in the jazz waltz genre, with descending diatonic arpeggios, in the key of B♭ major. Have fun with the articulations.

FRI

Workout #12 **Drum Tracks:** 10–12 **Type:** Lick **Genre:** 12/8 Blues

Today's etude is a commonly used blues lick in D major. Accent the first note, then slur the rest together.

SAT

Workout #13 **Drum Tracks:** 23, 30 **Type:** Rhythm **Genre:** Latin

Rhythms are usually the hardest musical concept for young players to grasp. The only way to really become comfortable with them is to listen to as many recordings as possible in the style you are attempting to play. (Practicing is necessary, too, of course.) If you are playing Latin jazz, you need to become a fan of Latin jazz. The Internet has made excuses virtually obsolete, since one can instantly find examples of almost any musician since the beginning of recorded music. Here is a typical Latin jazz rhythm in F and E♭, similar to the chord changes in "Tequila," as recorded by the Champs.

SUN

Workout #14 **Drum Tracks:** 24 **Type:** Rhythm **Genre:** Bossa Nova

Try your hand at these Latin rhythms in the key of G major. They have the same chord progression as the previous exercise.

MON

Workout #15   **Drum Tracks:** 13, 14, 16, 17   **Type:** Technique   **Genre:** Rock/Funk

Let's use the B major scale and concentrate on the low register of the sax. Try playing this workout as softly as possible. The low register doesn't usually speak very easily on the saxophone, so just do the best you can with the volume.

TUE

Workout #16   **Drum Tracks:** 19–21   **Type:** Pattern/Lick   **Genre:** Jazz Waltz

This lick in B♭ major contains two patterns: the first one goes 5-1, 5-2, 5-3, 5-4. The second one jumps down a 5th and then a 4th. The rhythms used in this week's exercises will start to get a little more challenging than they have been.

WED

Workout #17   **Drum Tracks:** 25   **Type:** Lick   **Genre:** Reggae

This D minor reggae lick is similar to what you might hear in a song from reggae artists like Bob Marley or Peter Tosh.

THU

Workout #18   **Drum Tracks:** 17, 18   **Type:** Lick/Technique   **Genre:** Rock/Funk

The blues scale is featured in this funk lick in G major. It is inspired by the horn lines of James Brown's band. Such phrases have heavily influenced all subsequent funk and soul bands.

FRI

Workout #19   **Drum Tracks:** 29, 30   **Type:** Lick   **Genre:** Latin

The time gets turned around on measure 3 in this B minor lick. It will feel strange at first, if you're doing it correctly.

SAT

Workout #20   **Drum Tracks:** 13, 16, 17   **Type:** Pattern   **Genre:** Rock/Funk

In this E minor funk lick, the time gets turned around once again.
Hint: Just read the music; don't let your ear steer you in the wrong direction.

SUN

Workout #21   **Drum Tracks:** 29   **Type:** Lick   **Genre:** Latin

To end a week full of rhythmic challenges, here is your weekly rhythm exercise – in E♭ major. Observe the phrasing.

WEEK 4

MON

Workout #22 **Drum Tracks:** 14, 15 **Type:** Pattern **Genre:** Rock

This is an A major scale in ascending and descending diatonic 3rds, using the up-up pattern. The phrasing is in groups of three.

TUE

Workout #23 **Drum Tracks:** 19–21 **Type:** Technique **Genre:** Jazz Waltz

It's not easy to slur octaves on the saxophone, and if you're a beginner, or even intermediate player, this exercise in C major may be a bit of a challenge. Try not to change your embouchure during this exercise, and let your voice box do most of the work.

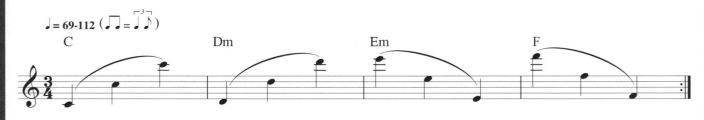

WED

Workout #24 **Drum Tracks:** 27, 28 **Type:** Technique **Genre:** New Orleans 2nd Line

In this exercise we see some short falls. To achieve a good sound on these you will have to use a combination of dropping your jaw and playing a quick descending scale, diatonic or chromatic, just a few notes. At the same time, diminuendo quickly in order to play the next note in time. In measure 1, you have some time to do a longer fall. The falls in measure 3 and 4 should be lip falls (jaw drop only).

THU

Workout #25　　　**Drum Tracks:** 13–15　　　**Type:** Pattern/Technique　　　**Genre:** Rock

These are longer, diatonic falls (glissandos) in the key of C, using the blues scale. The technique you should use is a quick descending scale with little or no jaw movement; at the same time, diminuendo quickly. Sometimes long falls are supposed to be really long, often lasting for a few measures or more. The long falls in this workout have to be finished before you get to the next note, so don't fall for too long.

FRI

Workout #26　　　**Drum Tracks:** 27, 28　　　**Type:** Technique　　　**Genre:** New Orleans 2nd Line

Today we'll play a mixture of short and long falls in the key of G.

SAT

Workout #27　　　**Drum Tracks:** 13–15　　　**Type:** Lick　　　**Genre:** Rock

Here is a funk lick in A minor using staccato and legato articulations. It's meant to be played slowly.

SUN

Workout #28　　　**Drum Tracks:** 19–21　　　**Type:** Pattern　　　**Genre:** Jazz Waltz

This rhythmic workout is a D major scale in ascending diatonic 4ths using the down-down pattern.

WEEK 5

MON

Workout #29   **Drum Tracks:** 28   **Type:** Lick   **Genre:** New Orleans 2nd Line

In this G major New Orleans 2nd Line rhythm lick, play any unmarked notes legato (long). Grace notes should be tongued, and then quickly slurred into the notes to which they are attached.

TUE

Workout #30   **Drum Tracks:** 1–3   **Type:** Lick   **Genre:** Swing

This lick in F major has some early jazz references in it. Musicians in the early days of American popular music, playing what ended up being called jazz, outlined major 6th and dominant 9th chords in their improvised solos. At that time, these chords sounded quite modern. The chord progression here: F6 for the first two measures, and C9 for measures 3 and 4.

WED

Workout #31   **Drum Tracks:** 16–18   **Type:** Rhythm   **Genre:** Funk

Here is a funky rhythm lick in D major designed to help you recognize 16th-note figures. We learn how to sight read intricate rhythms through recognition and repetition. The second half of this exercise is almost the same as the first half, starting an eighth note early.

THU

Workout #32   **Drum Tracks:** 19–21   **Type:** Pattern/Lick   **Genre:** Jazz Waltz

This lick in C major uses a common pentatonic scale pattern. It jumps diatonically in intervals of 4ths and 3rds. The phrasing splits each 3/4 measure into two groups of three.

FRI

Workout #33   **Drum Tracks:** 29, 30   **Type:** Rhythm   **Genre:** Latin

This C major exercise demonstrates the chord progression C–Am–F–G, which is known as the I–vi–IV–V progression. This was a common progression used in countless popular songs of the 1950s. Pay particular attention to the articulations.

SAT

Workout #34   **Drum Tracks:** 26   **Type:** Rhythm/Technique   **Genre:** Ska

Ska music is difficult to explain. The term encompasses a wide range of music styles. It could be described as a faster, rock-influenced version of reggae music. Both reggae and ska originated in Jamaica. Even though ska music is quick-paced, these lines should be played in a laid-back style.

SUN

Workout #35   **Drum Tracks:** 16–18   **Type:** Pattern   **Genre:** Funk

These F major staccato horn lines are inspired by the funk group Tower of Power. The falls in the second measure should be played short, not long, with little or no key usage and a quick diminuendo. Like their upward counterparts, downward grace notes (measure 2, beat 4) should be tongued and slurred into the following note.

MON

Workout #36   **Drum Tracks:** 13, 14   **Type:** Technique   **Genre:** Rock

This is a vibrato exercise only, with no articulation. There are at least two different ways to produce vibrato with the saxophone. This is a modified version of the classical method, although true classical vibrato is very subtle and constant. Outside the classical realm, you can use vibrato any way you want. Make very light up-and-down jaw movements. It should feel the same as saying "vah vah vah."

TUE

Workout #37   **Drum Tracks:** 13–15   **Type:** Scale/Pattern   **Genre:** Rock

The major pentatonic scale (1-2-3-5-6) is a simple scale that can be used in many complicated ways. Because it only has five notes (most scales and modes have seven notes), it's relatively easy to remember. It is a good way to get started improvising. This is a common pentatonic pattern in G major that reveals the five (unnamed) modes of the major pentatonic scale. The fifth mode of the pentatonic scale is used for playing over minor chords. In this case, the fifth mode is in E minor.

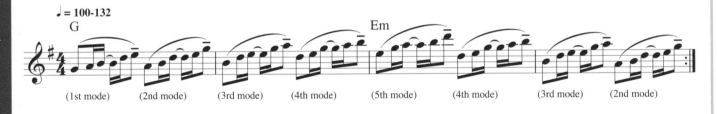

WED

Workout #38   **Drum Tracks:** 1, 2, 4, 5   **Type:** Technique   **Genre:** Swing

Scoops are an important part of jazz styling. Scooping is done with the laryngeal and jaw movement, not key movement (grace notes). Approach the note from about a half step below, fingering the written note. To accomplish this inflection, drop your jaw slightly and form the vowel sound "aw" with your mouth, and gradually tighten your embouchure and form the vowel sound "ee" to get the note in tune ("aw-ee").

THU

Workout #39   **Drum Tracks:** 19–21   **Type:** Scale   **Genre:** Jazz Waltz

This exercise demonstrates the A blues scale. It is easy to overuse this scale. It works quite well in blues, rock, and funk styles. It does not work well, generally, on standard tunes like "All the Things You Are" (Jerome Kern and Oscar Hammerstein II), or "A Nightingale Sang in Berkeley Square" (Eric Maschwitz and Manning Sherwin), because those songs use major scale harmony. You could use this A blues scale (1-♭3-4-♭5-5-♭7) when you see an A7 chord.

FRI

Workout #40   **Drum Tracks:** 19–21   **Type:** Scale/Pattern   **Genre:** Jazz Waltz

If the G pentatonic scale sounds oriental, that's because many oriental music genres use the pentatonic scale. The first two measures of this workout may also sound a bit like church chimes, which are often tuned to pentatonic scales. Regardless of these treatments, this pentatonic pattern is similar to a lick played by the great Motown saxophonist Junior Walker, among many other rock, soul, and jazz musicians.

SAT

Workout #41   **Drum Tracks:** 2, 5   **Type:** Technique   **Genre:** Swing

Now we're going to learn how to play note-to-note glissandos. We do that by slurring from one note to the next, playing all the "necessary" notes in between. You can play diatonically the notes in the scale indicated by the key signature (A♭, in this case), or chromatically, or a combination of both, from the beginning note to its "goal" note. You can eventually add a little mouth and/or jaw movement (scoop) to make the run smoother. If you want to hear the correct way to play glissandos, listen to Charlie Parker, Cannonball Adderley, or Phil Woods.

SUN

Workout #42   **Drum Tracks:** 22–24   **Type:** Scale/Technique   **Genre:** Bossa Nova

Here are some diatonic octave jumps in E major. The notes with closer intervals are slurred. Hold all notes for their full value.

Hint: In measure 4, it's okay to hold down the G♯ key while playing the low F♯. There are lots of instances where this is acceptable; you'll have to experiment with it on your own.

WEEK 7

MON

Workout #43 **Drum Tracks:** 25 **Type:** Technique **Genre:** Reggae

Let's start the week with a workout for the lower register of the saxophone, in the key of B♭ major.

TUE

Workout #44 **Drum Tracks:** 25 **Type:** Technique **Genre:** Reggae

In this exercise in E♭ major, we'll be concentrating on the upper register, especially the palm keys (high D, E♭, E, and F).

WED

Workout #45 **Drum Tracks:** 1, 2, 4, 5 **Type:** Technique **Genre:** Swing

In this melody, you'll see some runs indicated by a straight line from one note to another. These are quick glissandos, so just play diatonic notes (within the A major scale) between the start and end points.

Hint: The pickups to measure 1 are written out the way these runs are supposed to sound.

THU

Workout #46   **Drum Tracks:** 1, 2, 4, 5   **Type:** Technique   **Genre:** Swing

This melody has some offbeat turns in it. The way it's done in jazz is to hold the note almost full value, and right before you go to the next written note, go up diatonically (in the G major scale) to the next note and back. In measure 2, the turn is written out for you. In measure 3, you'll have to figure it out or listen to the recorded example.

FRI

Workout #47   **Drum Tracks:** 1, 2, 4, 5   **Type:** Technique   **Genre:** Swing

Here are some up and down runs in F major. The first one is written out for you.

SAT

Workout #48   **Drum Tracks:** 16–18   **Type:** Lick   **Genre:** Funk

This is a funky staccato exercise in D minor, inspired by the horn lines of Earth, Wind & Fire's "Getaway."

SUN

Workout #49   **Drum Tracks:** 22, 23, 29, 30   **Type:** Technique/Lick   **Genre:** Latin

Turns will show up in every style of music. In the jazz genre, turns are generally played as diatonic triplets. Here we have two turns starting on downbeats. The first turn in this workout (in measure 2) is written out, the second one is notated the way you will almost always see it written.

MON

Workout #50   **Drum Tracks:** 2, 3   **Type:** Technique/Rhythm   **Genre:** Swing

In this exercise in G major, use the Right Side Key 2 (rsk 2) to play the B-C-B triplets. As always, observe the phrase markings. In jazz phrasing, a general rule is to slur into and through triplets, tonguing again on the next available upbeat.

Right Side Key 2 (B to C trill)

TUE

Workout #51   **Drum Tracks:** 22, 23   **Type:** Technique   **Genre:** Bossa Nova

The front F key makes jumping from a high C to a high F very easy. Use the fingering for a high C (with the octave key) and add the front F key, which is located just above the B key in your left hand on your sax. The high F should pop out easily.

Front High F

WED

Workout #52   **Drum Tracks:** 13–15   **Type:** Scale/Technique   **Genre:** Rock

Here we see a little bit more advanced sax technique. You'll most likely hear it called a "lip down," "lip gliss," or "bend." Most of the time it is notated as it is here, with lines and slurs connecting the notes. Usually, you should employ your larynx (voice box) to bend these notes, not your lip or your jaw. Your jaw will move a little to help stabilize the reed, but it is your larynx that controls pitch. The scale used is for this exercise is a B whole tone scale. True to its name, this scale is comprised only of whole steps.

THU

Workout #53   **Drum Tracks:** 4–6   **Type:** Lick/Pattern   **Genre:** Swing

Quartal harmony is a useful tool in jazz, especially in the style from the late 1950s and early '60s called "hard bop." Saxophonists of the hard bop era include Joe Henderson, Jackie McLean, John Coltrane, and Wayne Shorter. The lick below uses quartal chords (triads of perfect 4ths) in first and second inversions, played mostly in whole steps.

FRI

Workout #54   **Drum Tracks:** 19–21   **Type:** Pattern   **Genre:** Jazz Waltz

These G major scale arpeggio patterns are in 3/4 time. On the turnaround, the sequence mutates and becomes an example of "over the bar" playing, a method of improvising in which melodies are not bound by musical parameters such as bar lines, chord structure, or song form.

SAT

Workout #55   **Drum Tracks:** 1, 4   **Type:** Scale   **Genre:** Swing

This D♭ major scale lick is a workout for the lower register of the horn and will help you get more familiar with the table keys of the left hand. Swing the eighth notes with a triplet feel.

SUN

Workout #56   **Drum Tracks:** 23, 29, 30   **Type:** Rhythm/Lick   **Genre:** Latin

Here is a lick in F major containing various rhythms. It further demonstrates how to phrase triplets in jazz and Latin jazz.

21

WEEK 9

MON

Workout #57 **Drum Tracks:** 1–3 **Type:** Technique **Genre:** Swing

Here is a bebop lick in C with some phrasing, articulations, and inflections we've covered so far.

TUE

Workout #58 **Drum Tracks:** 22–24 **Type:** Pattern/Rhythm **Genre:** Bossa Nova

The rhythms in this D major exercise are typical of what you'll encounter in Latin styles of music. You won't always have articulations written in this thoroughly. They are included here so that, through recognition and repetition, you can remember the correct phrasing when it isn't provided for you.

WED

Workout #59 **Drum Tracks:** 26 **Type:** Rhythm **Genre:** Ska

In this Ska rhythm exercise, also in D major, you should start slowly, and speed up your metronome over time until you're comfortable with it at a bright tempo.

THU

Workout #60 **Drum Tracks:** 29, 30 **Type:** Lick/Technique **Genre:** Latin

Today's exercise is a bebop lick in F major over a Latin groove. Even though you've played licks like this in a swing style before, play straight-eighth notes. The first turn is written out for you.

FRI

Workout #61 **Drum Tracks:** 27 **Type:** Rhythm/Technique **Genre:** New Orleans 2nd Line

This exercise in B♭ major has some opposing rhythms that may throw you off. Add the left hand palm D or E♭ (or both, depending on the intonation you want) to the D♭ in measure 2 for the trill fingering. Trills are usually diatonic, but in this case you could play a chromatic, diatonic or even quarter-tone trill, in order to give the turn a bluesy feel.

Palm D trill (C♯ to D)

SAT

Workout #62 **Drum Tracks:** 25 **Type:** Rhythm **Genre:** Reggae

Reggae incorporates several different styles of music: Latin, bebop, funk, rock, et al. In this D major exercise you may recognize these rhythms from other styles, but the phrasing is slightly different. Because the music is slower and eighth notes are played straight, odd combinations of articulations are frequently used.

SUN

Workout #63 **Drum Tracks:** 7–9 **Type:** Rhythm **Genre:** Shuffle

Triplet-feel swing is a critical concept to grasp in the jazz idiom. In this E♭ major exercise, the triplets all end with an articulated note that demonstrates where following upbeats should land, rhythmically speaking.

MON

Workout #64   **Drum Tracks:** 10–12   **Type:** Lick/Pattern   **Genre:** 12/8 Blues

This is a common blues lick in E. 12/8 meter is often used in lieu of 4/4 meter if a composition has a slow triplet feel throughout.

TUE

Workout #65   **Drum Tracks:** 4–6   **Type:** Lick/Pattern   **Genre:** Swing

Tuesday's lick utilizes A major triads, in various inversions, alternating with corresponding triads a tritone away (E♭). The two triads are connected with lead tones.

WED

Workout #66   **Drum Tracks:** 4–6   **Type:** Lick   **Genre:** Swing

This lick in D follows a progression often used by Count Basie in the 1930s and '40s. The second half of this exercise highlights the sixth and the ninth degrees of the D major scale. The bend articulation in measure 4 is an alternate notation for a scoop.

THU

Workout #67   **Drum Tracks:** 23, 29   **Type:** Lick   **Genre:** Latin

The following lick follows a common progression in popular music in which the top note of a minor chord descends chromatically.

FRI

Workout #68   **Drum Tracks:** 2, 3, 28   **Type:** Lick   **Genre:** Swing

In the first measure of this lick, we'll be outlining two octaves of an E♭maj7 chord, starting with the lead tones (7th). The rest of the exercise is a passing-tone workout following the notated chord progression. However, a lick like this would usually be played over four measures of one chord (E♭maj7).

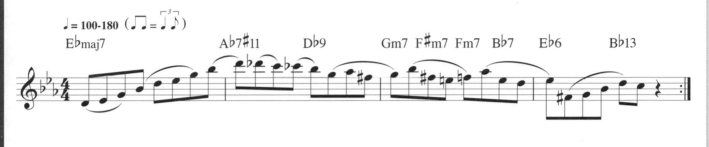

SAT

Workout #69   **Drum Tracks:** 3, 4, 7, 8   **Type:** Pattern   **Genre:** Shuffle/Swing

This triplet pattern sounds more classical than jazz, but bebop founding father Charlie Parker often played something similar in some of his most famous solos. The lick outlines a Dm chord in different inversions, and utilizes much of the saxophone's range.

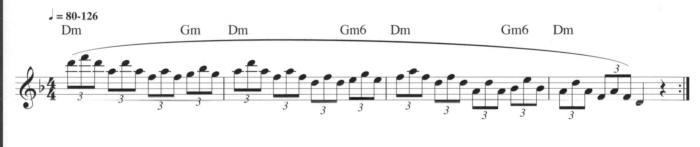

SUN

Workout #70   **Drum Tracks:** 22, 23, 29, 30   **Type:** Lick   **Genre:** Latin

Today's A minor lick is a rhythm exercise. To get a feel for this type of music, listen to some Afro-Cuban jazz before you try it yourself. (Mongo Santamaria, Cal Tjader, Dizzy Gillespie, et al. You can find several examples on YouTube.)

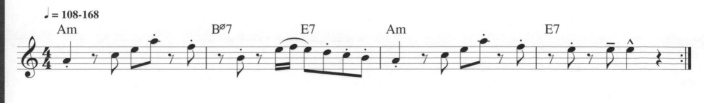

WEEK 11

MON

Workout #71   **Drum Tracks:** 1, 2, 4, 5   **Type:** Lick/Pattern   **Genre:** Swing

The week's first lick uses 7-5-3-1 descending arpeggios. It would work well over F♯ minor or A major. Some offset triplets are thrown in to keep it interesting.

TUE

Workout #72   **Drum Tracks:** 22–24, 29, 30   **Type:** Lick/Pattern   **Genre:** Bossa Nova

This lick outlines a Bm9 chord, dipping down to lead tones and back, followed by diatonic passing tones between each partial. Use the F♯ trill fingering where indicated.

Note: The F♯ trill key is located just below and to the right of the middle finger F♯ key in your right hand (below the high F♯ key on some horns). Add the F♯ trill key to an F to achieve the trill.

Note: This fingering is optional, but its usage will make some passages easier to play. Determining when to use it will become automatic after many hours of practice.

F♯/G♭ Trill Key

WED

Workout #73   **Drum Tracks:** 1–3   **Type:** Pattern   **Genre:** Swing

Here is a D minor 2-1-7-1, 3-2-1-2, etc. scalar exercise that ascends diatonically. The lowest note in each four-note pattern is a lead tone (a half step below the second diatonic note).

THU

Workout #74   **Drum Tracks:** 2, 3, 5, 6, 28   **Type:** Pattern   **Genre:** Swing

This D major pattern outlines diatonically descending 7-5-3-1 arpeggios, approached from a half step below (leading tone).

FRI

Workout #75   **Drum Tracks:** 1–3, 8, 9, 28   **Type:** Lick   **Genre:** Swing

Try this blues lick in B dominant (B7) that uses the interval of diatonic 6ths. The chord progression is B7–E7–F#7 (I–IV–V). This difficult saxophone key is not uncommon in the blues genre.

SAT

Workout #76   **Drum Tracks:** 2, 5   **Type:** Pattern   **Genre:** Swing

Lead tones, which lead into "goal" tones, are an important tool in improvising. They are used in creating and connecting musical ideas. This pattern in F major (1-7-2-1, 2-1-3-2, etc.) substitutes the second note in each four-note pattern with a lead tone.

SUN

Workout #77   **Drum Tracks:** 14, 15   **Type:** Rhythm   **Genre:** Rock

This lick in G major is all upbeats, using elements of the blues scale and lead tones. Funk saxophonists such as Maceo Parker play on the upbeats so much that it's almost shocking when they start playing on downbeats. These end-of-the-week rhythms will continue to get gradually more difficult as we progress through the year.

MON

Workout #78   **Drum Tracks:** 14, 15   **Type:** Pattern/Technique   **Genre:** Rock

These are chromatically ascending minor 3rds, except for the last measure, which are tritones descending in minor 3rds. This pattern is an essential tool for connecting and creating ideas during improvisation. You will also find this pattern used in classical saxophone repertoire. Observe the back-tonguing, and play straight eighth notes.

TUE

Workout #79   **Drum Tracks:** 4   **Type:** Scale/Pattern   **Genre:** Swing

This workout uses the diminished scale, which we'll discuss in more depth throughout this book. Here is the G diminished scale ascending and descending on measures 1 and 3. Measure 2 has ascending 3rds descending diatonically, and measure 4 has exactly the opposite pattern.

WED

Workout #80   **Drum Tracks:** 19   **Type:** Pattern/Rhythm   **Genre:** Swing

This is a rhythm exercise in which 16th notes will be played straight over the swinging jazz waltz. In the key of E major, you'll be playing descending and ascending diatonic 3rds in the up-up pattern.

THU

Workout #81   **Drum Tracks:** 10   **Type:** Pattern/Technique   **Genre:** 12/8 Ballad

Today's diatonic pattern follows the written chord progression. The interval will be either a diatonic 5th or 6th within the A major scale. It will also work the low register of the horn, which is the foundation of each sax player's unique sound.

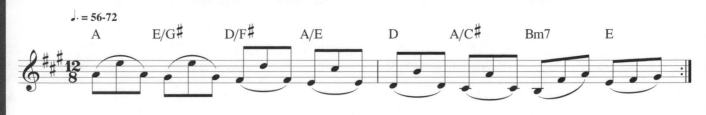

FRI

Workout #82   **Drum Tracks:** 27, 28   **Type:** Rhythm   **Genre:** New Orleans 2nd Line

In this D major exercise, you'll find some rhythms and phrasing intrinsic to the New Orleans style, most of which stem from the music of trumpeter and singer Louis Armstrong, the Father of Jazz.

SAT

Workout #83   **Drum Tracks:** 24, 30   **Type:** Rhythm   **Genre:** Latin

Here are some Latin rhythms in A♭ major.

SUN

Workout #84   **Drum Tracks:** 17–18   **Type:** Rhythm   **Genre:** Funk

These are some typical funk horn lines in F major. Observe all articulations.

29

MON

Workout #85 **Drum Tracks:** 22, 23 **Type:** Scale **Genre:** Bossa Nova

All seven modes of the major scale are used in Western music. We've already been using two of them. The major scale is also known as the Ionian mode. Another mode we've already seen a few times is the natural minor scale, or Aeolian mode (sixth degree of a major scale). Modes are degrees of the same scale, in this case, degrees of the F major scale. This is a C Mixolydian mode. The C Mixolydian mode is essentially an F major scale starting on the fifth degree.

TUE

Workout #86 **Drum Tracks:** 26 **Type:** Rhythm **Genre:** Ska

Today's intermediate rhythms employ the G Dorian mode (the second degree of the F major scale). The Dorian mode is similar to a natural minor scale (Aeolian mode), but the sixth degree of the Dorian mode will be natural, not flat.

WED

Workout #87 **Drum Tracks:** 16–18 **Type:** Technique **Genre:** Funk

In this exercise in D minor (Dorian mode: refer to key signature), we'll be concentrating specifically on the highest conventional saxophone notes. There are even higher notes that the saxophone is capable of playing, which are in the altissimo range. (We'll get to that later.)

Workout #88   **Drum Tracks:** 7–9   **Type:** Technique   **Genre:** Shuffle

Let's practice another workout for the low range of the saxophone, using chromatic phrases in B♭ major.

Workout #89   **Drum Tracks:** 4–6   **Type:** Pattern   **Genre:** Swing

Measures 1 and 2 of this exercise are perfect 4ths ascending in major 2nds in an up-up pattern. Measures 3 and 4 use the down-down pattern. Notice the lack of a key signature; this is an atonal pattern.

Workout #90   **Drum Tracks:** 13,14   **Type:** Pattern   **Genre:** Rock

Here are some diatonic 5ths in D major, ascending in an alternating down-up pattern.

Workout #91   **Drum Tracks:** 22   **Type:** Pattern   **Genre:** 12/8 Ballad

During improvisation, the Mixolydian mode can also be used over suspended (sus) chords. A G13sus arpeggio would definitely not include the third degree of the Mixolydian mode. However, this G mixolydian pattern includes the third, which sounds just fine when used as a passing tone over the G13sus chord.

MON

Workout #92 **Drum Tracks:** 13, 14 **Type:** Pattern **Genre:** Rock

Arpeggios can be used in the same fashion for all modes of a scale. These arpeggios, in an up-down alternating pattern, all have the same tonality as D major (demonstrated in measure 4).

TUE

Workout #93 **Drum Tracks:** 19–21 **Type:** Pattern **Genre:** Jazz Waltz

This exercise demonstrates the quartal properties of the Cycle of 4ths. Here, all 12 notes of the chromatic scale are used in 3/4 time over four measures. Also, each measure contains a quartal chord (composed of perfect 4ths) and each successive measure ascends by a minor 3rd.

WED

Workout #94 **Drum Tracks:** 2, 3 **Type:** Pattern **Genre:** Swing

A diminished scale is a symmetrical scale with a pattern that alternates whole and half steps. When it starts on a whole step (for use over diminished chords), the sequence is W-H-W-H-W-H-W-H. In this E diminished exercise, the pattern in measures 1 and 2 is descending diatonic 2nds ascending diatonically. In measures 3 and 4, the pattern is reversed, with ascending diatonic 2nds descending diatonically.

Workout #95　　　**Drum Tracks:** 1–3　　　**Type:** Pattern　　　**Genre:** Swing

Augmented chords usually resolve to a I (tonic) chord, similar to dominant (V7) chords. Here we have alternating augmented arpeggios ascending in whole tones, eventually descending back to the tonic (C).

Workout #96　　　**Drum Tracks:** 27, 28　　　**Type:** Pattern　　　**Genre:** New Orleans 2nd Line

These are diatonic 7ths in the key of E major ascending and descending in diatonic 3rds.

Workout #97　　　**Drum Tracks:** 29　　　**Type:** Pattern　　　**Genre:** Latin

These 10ths (an octave plus a 3rd) ascend diatonically in the key of D♭ major. Yes, we'll be covering all keys. Take it slowly.

Workout #98　　　**Drum Tracks:** 25　　　**Type:** Pattern　　　**Genre:** Reggae

Practice these chromatic triplet figures that alternate between minor 3rds and tritones. There are basically only three diminished scales, because each diminished scale contains three others: Every note of a diminished arpeggio is the start of another diminished scale. The D diminished scale also contains the F, A♭, and B diminished scales.

MON

Workout #99   **Drum Tracks:** 4–6   **Type:** Pattern   **Genre:** Swing

Diminished scales and patterns work well over #9 (altered) chords. Here is a G diminished pattern (perfect 4ths in alternating up-down minor 3rds) that works well over this G7#9 chord.

TUE

Workout #100   **Drum Tracks:** 29   **Type:** Pattern **Genre:** Latin

The first half of this E major arpeggio pattern has written-out turns, while in the second half, you're given only a turn symbol.

WED

Workout #101   **Drum Tracks:** 10–12   **Type:** Pattern   **Genre:** 12/8

Make sure you get the 12/8 feel in your head before attempting this G diminished pattern.

Workout #102 **Drum Tracks:** 19–21 **Type:** Lick/Rhythm **Genre:** Jazz Waltz

In the first half of this F♯ minor exercise, the articulations are written in for you. In the second half, you see the expression *sim.* (an abbreviation of *simile*), which means "play similar articulations until otherwise noted."

Workout #103 **Drum Tracks:** 28 **Type:** Rhythm/Lick **Genre:** New Orleans 2nd Line

In this B♭ major exercise, we have some falls, a turn, and a chromatic jazz lick.

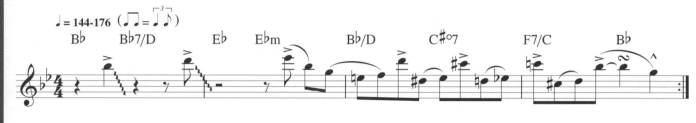

Workout #104 **Drum Tracks:** 16–18 **Type:** Rhythm **Genre:** Funk

This tricky rhythm is in D Dorian. Parliament, a funk group from the 1970s, played a lot of these types of horn lines – featuring the world's funkiest alto saxophonist, Maceo Parker.

Workout #105 **Drum Tracks:** 30 **Type:** Pattern **Genre:** Latin

Here is your Latin-flavored rhythm workout for the week, in B minor.

SAXOPHONE AEROBICS

WEEK 16

MON

Workout #106   **Drum Tracks:** 25   **Type:** Pattern   **Genre:** Reggae

In this B minor (Aeolian) exercise, 1-3-5-8 arpeggios descend diatonically to the V chord (F#).

TUE

Workout #107   **Drum Tracks:** 26   **Type:** Rhythm   **Genre:** Ska

You'll relish this E minor rhythm lick and its abundant articulation.

WED

Workout #108   **Drum Tracks:** 28   **Type:** Lick/Technique   **Genre:** New Orleans 2nd Line

This exercise is a jazz lick in C with typical New Orleans-style phrasing.

Note: The turn in measure 4 should be diatonic, so you should go up to D, not C#. Use palm Eb (from Workout #61).

THU

Workout #109   Drum Tracks: 23, 24   Type: Pattern   Genre: Bossa Nova

A diminished scale starting with a half step is the correct scale to use over a dominant ♭9 chord. Another way to think of C7♭9 is to play a D♭ diminished scale starting on C.

FRI

Workout #110   Drum Tracks: 14, 15   Type: Pattern   Genre: Rock

Altered chords (V#9) can be outlined a few different ways. One way to voice these chords is to use a 3-5-8-#9 arpeggio. Here is the descending version of this altered chord, played in descending major 2nds for an interesting harmonic effect.

SAT

Workout #111   Drum Tracks: 29   Type: Lick   Genre: Latin

It's easier to improvise in G# minor instead of its enharmonic equivalent, A♭ minor (Aeolian), because when one is making quick decisions during improvisation, five sharps (B major = G# minor) are much easier to manage than seven flats (C♭ major = A♭ minor).

SUN

Workout #112   Drum Tracks: 30   Type: Pattern   Genre: Latin

Here is another Latin workout in C# minor that has a sequential, upbeat-driven rhythm.

MON

Workout #113 **Drum Tracks:** 7–9 **Type:** Scale **Genre:** Shuffle

There are four bebop scales: major, dominant, Dorian, and melodic minor. I'll explain each of the bebop scales as we learn them individually. The bebop dominant scale is the most widely used bebop scale. Here is a bebop dominant scale and lick in the key of B♭. The first measure of this exercise demonstrates the descending version of this scale.

TUE

Workout #114 **Drum Tracks:** 1–3 **Type:** Scale/Lick **Genre:** Swing

This lick showcases the G bebop major scale, which is essentially a G major scale with a chromatic passing tone between the fifth and sixth notes of the scale (D#/E♭).

WED

Workout #115 **Drum Tracks:** 16–18 **Type:** Scale **Genre:** Funk

The bebop Dorian scale is simply a Dorian mode with an added passing tone between the third and fourth degrees of the scale. In this workout, the G bebop Dorian scale in measure 1 flows nicely through its corresponding C dominant (C7) chord. This is due to the fact that the G bebop Dorian scale and the C bebop dominant scale are the same scale, but starting on different degrees.

THU

Workout #116 **Drum Tracks:** 22–24 **Type:** Scale **Genre:** Bossa Nova

The Lydian mode is a major scale starting and ending on the fourth degree. In this case, observe that an E♭ Lydian mode is the same scale as a B♭ major scale (check the key signature). As explained in Workout #85, there are seven modes based off of the major scale, one for each note of the scale.

FRI

Workout #117 **Drum Tracks:** 19–21 **Type:** Pattern/Lick **Genre:** Jazz Waltz

In this exercise, the G pentatonic scale is played over an Fmaj7♭5 chord. The G pentatonic scale contains (in order) the 9th, 3rd, #4th, 6th, and 7th degrees of the F Lydian mode.

SAT

Workout #118 **Drum Tracks:** 16–18 **Type:** Pattern **Genre:** Funk

This Lydian quadratonic pattern can be treated like a pentatonic scale. In this case, the 7th, tonic, 3rd, and #4th are treated much like the modes of a pentatonic scale.

SUN

Workout #119 **Drum Tracks:** 4–6 **Type:** Pattern **Genre:** Swing

A Lydian tri-tonic pattern of the 3rd, #4th, and 7th can also be used like a pentatonic scale (played in modes), as demonstrated here.

WEEK 18

MON

Workout #120   **Drum Tracks:** 1–3   **Type:** Pattern   **Genre:** Swing

This type of alternating, descending diminished arpeggio pattern works well in the blues or bebop genre.

TUE

Workout #121   **Drum Tracks:** 22, 23   **Type:** Scale   **Genre:** Bossa Nova

As explained in Workout #109, the scale one would use for a dominant ♭9 chord is a diminished scale starting on the half step. This exercise demonstrates the A7♭9 diminished scale and arpeggio.

WED

Workout #122   **Drum Tracks:** 7–9   **Type:** Pattern/Lick   **Genre:** Shuffle

One of the most popular vehicles for jazz improvisation is the song "I Got Rhythm" by George and Ira Gershwin. The chord changes of that tune have been used for literally hundreds of bebop heads. The next five exercises will be based on the chord changes of the first four measures of "I Got Rhythm," often called "rhythm changes."

Note: The demo track is played on tenor sax.

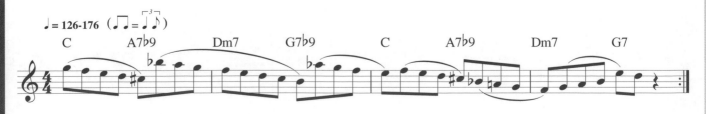

THU

Workout #123   **Drum Tracks:** 1–3   **Type:** Pattern/Lick   **Genre:** Swing

As in the previous exercise, this lick incorporates the A7♭9 diminished scale, and creates a sequence that leads back to the tonal center (C major).

Note: The demo track is played on tenor sax.

FRI

Workout #124   **Drum Tracks:** 24   **Type:** Pattern/Lick   **Genre:** Bossa Nova

Again, this is a "rhythm changes" lick using diminished scales, lead tones, and passing tones to create melodies.

Note: The demo track is played on tenor sax.

SAT

Workout #125   **Drum Tracks:** 4–6   **Type:** Pattern/Lick   **Genre:** Swing

Another bebop lick based on "rhythm changes" in G (major).

Note: The demo track is played on alto sax.

SUN

Workout #126   **Drum Tracks:** 29   **Type:** Pattern   **Genre:** Latin

Here is a Latin version of an excerpt from "rhythm changes." In keeping with our end-of-the-week rhythm workout routine, I've juxtaposed a triplet feel over a straight Latin beat, a technique that is inherent to Afro-Cuban music.

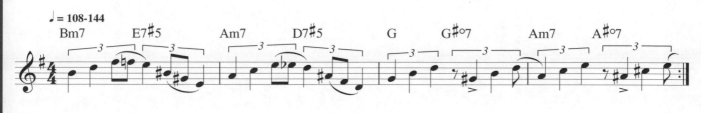

WEEK 19

MON

Workout #127   **Drum Tracks:** 2, 3   **Type:** Lick   **Genre:** Swing

The song "Cherokee" by Ray Noble has a popular chord progression on which to improvise. This exercise is based on an excerpt from the "A" section (verse) of "Cherokee" in the alto sax key. The lick used in the chord changes of measures 1 and 2 is mirrored to match the changes at measures 3 and 4, with the interval difference of a diatonic 4th.
Note: The demo track is played on alto sax.

TUE

Workout #128   **Drum Tracks:** 2, 3   **Type:** Lick   **Genre:** Swing

This workout has the same chord changes as the previous exercise ("Cherokee"), transposed for tenor sax. Again, the sequence in measures 1 and 2 is mirrored in measures 3 and 4, but the interval difference this time is up a diatonic 2nd.
Note: The demo track is played on tenor sax.

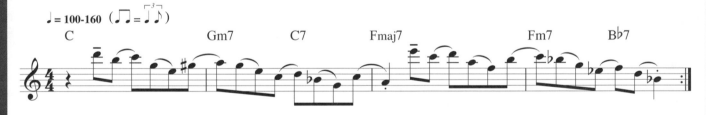

WED

Workout #129   **Drum Tracks:** 5, 6   **Type:** Lick   **Genre:** Swing

The bridge of "Cherokee" jumps up a minor 3rd from the verse and has several measures of ii–V–I progressions, which is a perfect vehicle for sequential improvisation. Here is an example of sequential playing over condensed chord changes of the bridge of "Cherokee" in the alto sax key.
Note: The demo track is played on alto sax.

THU

Workout #130 **Drum Tracks:** 23, 24 **Type:** Scale/Technique **Genre:** Bossa Nova

Transposed for tenor sax, this exercise shows how to create scalar, diatonic lines over the bridge of "Cherokee," starting on any diatonic note. The last note is optional: At a very fast tempo you may be able to repeat this etude in one (big) breath.

Note: The demo track is played on tenor sax.

FRI

Workout #131 **Drum Tracks:** 27, 28 **Type:** Pattern **Genre:** New Orleans 2nd Line

The chord changes of "Woodyn't You?" by Dizzy Gillespie also have a lot of descending ii–Vs, using ø7 and ♭9 chords. Here we have an open-voiced (wide intervals) sequence (1-5-7-10) that is mirrored in the changes of every measure. This example is based on a Sonny Rollins lick from *Live at the Village Vanguard*.

Note: The demo track is played on alto sax.

SAT

Workout #132 **Drum Tracks:** 8, 9 **Type:** Pattern **Genre:** Shuffle

This time we'll be playing the same chord progression from "Woodyn't You?" transposed for tenor sax. The close-voiced (narrow intervals) sequence used here occurs over a two-measure phrase and is repeated in the following two measures.

Note: The demo track is played on tenor sax.

SUN

Workout #133 **Drum Tracks:** 1, 2 **Type:** Pattern/Lick/Rhythm **Genre:** Swing

In these intervallic sequences, each mirrored phrase is a diatonic step away from its predecessor. In measures 1 and 2, the descending Eb ø7 arpeggio (7-5-3-1), approached from a lead tone, is followed by the Ab7♭9 diminished arpeggio, a diatonic step away (3-9-7-5), also approached from a lead tone. Measures 3 and 4 have the same digital lick following the chord progression, with a rhythmic twist: The sequence starts an eighth note earlier. The changes have been transposed for alto sax.

Note: The demo track is played on alto sax.

43

MON

Workout #134   **Drum Tracks:** 26   **Type:** Pattern   **Genre:** Ska

This week, we'll be working on some more saxophone techniques. It is important that a saxophonist be able to scoop and bend notes by using a combination of laryngeal and jaw adjustment, while at the same time trying not to change the embouchure (mouth position). Being able to scoop and bend notes will improve your intonation as well as enhance your sound and expressivity. In this exercise, dip to the slurred notes without changing fingerings. This is only a half step, people. You can do it! By the end of this week we'll be dipping down a minor 3rd.

TUE

Workout #135   **Drum Tracks:** 23, 24   **Type:** Pattern   **Genre:** Bossa Nova

Today's exercise demonstrates how much easier it can be to read abbreviated turn symbols than to read written-out turns.

Hint: Use the F♯ trill fingering to perform the turn on the "and" of beat 3 in the third measure.

WED

Workout #136   **Drum Tracks:** 27, 28   **Type:** Pattern   **Genre:** New Orleans 2nd Line

These runs (glissandos) are in D dominant. Remember: When you see a turn symbol, go up to the next diatonic note (one within the current tonality or scale) and back down to the original note before proceeding in time to the next written note. Legato tongue the unmarked notes.

THU

Workout #137   **Drum Tracks:** 13   **Type:** Pattern   **Genre:** Rock

It's been a while since we've done a workout for the high register of the horn. So, here is a workout in F major that goes up to high F♮. We'll be playing up to high F♯ by the end of the week.

FRI

Workout #138   **Drum Tracks:** 16, 17   **Type:** Pattern   **Genre:** Funk

Here are some dips down a major 2nd and scoops back up to the tonic. "Feel" the passing half steps, but make smooth transitions from note to note (*portamento*).

Note: This one is tough. The pitches don't have to be perfect, and it's okay if it sounds bad, but strive for some semblance of perfection.

SAT

Workout #139   **Drum Tracks:** 8   **Type:** Pattern   **Genre:** Shuffle

Today let's work on minor 3rd dips and scoops. Again, this exercise doesn't have to be perfectly in tune. It's a little faster than Workout #138, just to save you from some mental anguish. The slower you play this one, the harder it is.

SUN

Workout #140   **Drum Tracks:** 22, 23   **Type:** Pattern/Rhythm   **Genre:** Bossa Nova

Okay, here are those high F♯s mentioned on Thursday. If you have a high F♯ key, that's great, but if you don't, no worries. The fingering is easy: On alto, play a C with the octave key, add the front F key and rsk 1 (right side key 1). The fingering for tenor is the same, except you'll probably have to add the F key with your right index finger if the note is flat.

MON

Workout #141   **Drum Tracks:** 2, 3   **Type:** Pattern   **Genre:** Swing

This week we'll be studying the harmony of John Coltrane, indisputably one of the most important musicians of the 20th century. In the late 1950s, he perfected his "sheets of sound" technique, in which he played flurries of notes over ballads and medium tempos, while at very fast tempos he was able to make difficult runs seem effortless. Coltrane's practice regimen is legendary. It is often said he would fall asleep and wake up with the horn in his mouth. His most famous composition is "Giant Steps," a beautiful, quick-paced composition, notorious for its difficult chord changes, which make for some awkward improvisation. This week, we'll take a close look at the harmony used in this tune and other Coltrane compositions like it. This first exercise is designed to demonstrate the matrix used in the chord changes for these compositions: up a minor 3rd, up a 4th. Here are the chord changes to first four measures of "Giant Steps" in the alto sax key.

Note: The demo track is played on alto sax.

TUE

Workout #142   **Drum Tracks:** 2, 3   **Type:** Pattern   **Genre:** Swing

John Coltrane used four-note patterns to create his landmark solo on "Giant Steps." This 1-3-5-3 digital workout utilizes major triads following the chord changes to the first four measures of "Giant Steps" in the tenor sax key.

Note: The demo track is played on tenor sax.

WED

Workout #143   **Drum Tracks:** 2, 23   **Type:** Pattern   **Genre:** Swing

While improvising on "Giant Steps," Coltrane repeated the 1-2-3-5 pattern several times. Here is that pattern played over the chord changes to the first four measures of "Giant Steps" in the alto sax key.

Note: The demo track is played on alto sax.

Workout #144　　　　**Drum Tracks:** 2, 3　　　　　　**Type:** Pattern　　　　　　**Genre:** Swing

There are two slightly more interesting patterns used in this exercise. In each measure, following the chord changes to the second four measures of "Giant Steps" (in the tenor sax key), the sequence goes 3-5-2-1, 5-7-3-5. (The last measure of this exercise has been "customized" in order to logically conclude the melody.)

Note: The demo track is played on tenor sax.

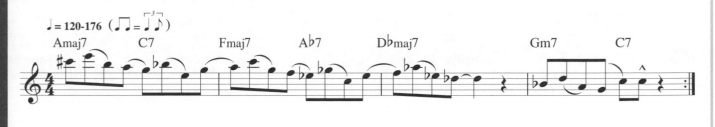

Workout #145　　　　**Drum Tracks:** 5, 6　　　　　　**Type:** Pattern　　　　　　**Genre:** Swing

This time we'll be playing an etude following the alto sax changes for the second four measures of "Giant Steps." For the most part, the digital sequence used is 3-5-8-7, 5-3-1-7.

Note: The demo track is played on alto sax.

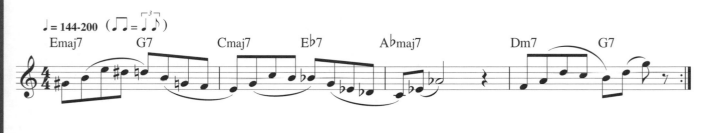

Workout #146　　　　**Drum Tracks:** 5, 6　　　　　　**Type:** Pattern　　　　　　**Genre:** Swing

This exercise is based on the reharmonized chord changes that Coltrane created from the standard jazz tune, "How High the Moon" (Morgan Lewis and Nancy Hamilton). His new composition, incorporating the "Coltrane Matrix," was called "Satellite." Here are the first four measures of that tune in the alto sax key. This exercise starts off with a 1-5-1-3 pattern. The second pattern in each measure deviates from diatonic tonality: 8-5-#11-3, in order to make a harmonically smooth turnaround into the tonic of the following measure.

Note: The demo track is played on alto sax.

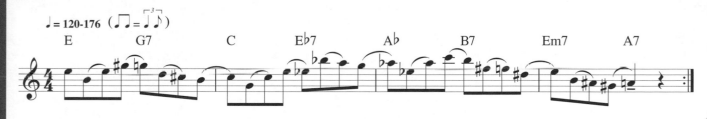

Workout #147　　　　**Drum Tracks:** 5, 6　　　　　　**Type:** Pattern　　　　　　**Genre:** Swing

For our rhythmic workout this week, here are some random patterns in groups of five eighth notes over an excerpt from the chord changes to "Satellite" in the tenor sax key.

Note: The demo track is played on tenor sax.

WEEK 22

MON

Workout #148   **Drum Tracks:** 4–6   **Type:** Rhythm   **Genre:** Swing

This week, we'll be doing rhythm workouts. This first exercise is an excerpt from the Cycle of 5ths. The rhythm is loosely based on Thelonious Monk's "Evidence."

TUE

Workout #149   **Drum Tracks:** 27, 28   **Type:** Rhythm   **Genre:** New Orleans 2nd Line

Here is another rhythm exercise in E major. You know what to do (more than just play the notes).

WED

Workout #150   **Drum Tracks:** 19–21   **Type:** Scale/Rhythm   **Genre:** Jazz Waltz

The melodic minor scale in classical theory is twofold: It has an ascending version and a descending version. In jazz theory, only the ascending version is used, and it has its own set of modes. We'll be covering those in the not-too-distant future. In this exercise, measures 1 and 2 demonstrate the F melodic minor ascending scale, while measures 3 and 4 demonstrate the descending version, which is really just a natural minor or Aeolian mode.

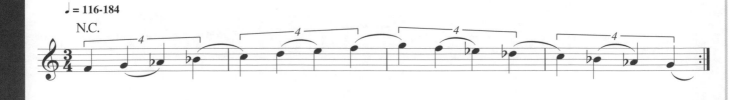

Workout #151   **Drum Tracks:** 10-12   **Type:** Rhythm   **Genre:** 12/8 Blues

Playing all of the accents, you should be able to hear quarter-note triplets in this A dominant rhythm workout.

Workout #152   **Drum Tracks:** 16–18   **Type:** Rhythm   **Genre:** Funk

This C Dorian exercise is based on the rhythm guitar part to "Mister Magic" by Grover Washington Jr.

Workout #153   **Drum Tracks:** 25   **Type:** Rhythm   **Genre:** Reggae

As in Workout #149, this rhythm is offset in the second half of the exercise. However, this time the notes in the first and second halves are almost identical, to make the sequence more obvious. (Key of C# minor.)

Workout #154   **Drum Tracks:** 1, 2   **Type:** Rhythm   **Genre:** Swing

This rhythm in B♭ major is the most advanced rhythm in this book so far. The rhythm of the phrase at measure 3 is exactly the same as the rhythm at measure 1, only it's offset by exactly one-third of a triplet. Good luck with this one! It probably won't feel right even if you play it correctly. I believe it forces you to use a dormant part of your brain.

Hint: Think of the beginning of measure 4 as a continuation of the offset triplets in measure 3, and concentrate on listening for beat 2 of measure 4 so you can nail the second eighth-note beat of the triplet.

MON

Workout #155 **Drum Tracks:** 4–6 **Type:** Technique **Genre:** Swing

For most of this week, we'll be studying major pentatonic scales and some of the different ways they are used in improvisation.

This workout is in the key of G minor using the B♭ pentatonic scale (1-2-3-5-6 of the B♭ major scale) in measures 1 and 3. Measures 2 and 4 are up a half step (B pentatonic). This is a common technique used for playing outside the changes.

TUE

Workout #156 **Drum Tracks:** 22–24 **Type:** Technique **Genre:** Bossa Nova

In this A♭ major exercise, the A♭ pentatonic scale is used in the first half of every measure, and an A pentatonic is used in the second half of every measure.

WED

Workout #157 **Drum Tracks:** 29 **Type:** Technique **Genre:** Latin

Here we have an A pentatonic over an F♯ minor chord in measure 1, jumping a tritone away to E♭ pentatonic in measure 2. Measures 3 and 4 switch from A pentatonic to E♭ pentatonic (a tritone apart) every two beats.

THU

Workout #158   Drum Tracks: 19–21   Type: Technique   Genre: Jazz Waltz

Today's workout is the "major" version of the same technique used in the previous exercise (pentatonics a tritone away). F pentatonics are mixed in with B pentatonics in this F major workout.

Note: Yes, the phrasing is meant to trip you up a little.

FRI

Workout #159   Drum Tracks: 26   Type: Scale   Genre: Ska

This is an F#/G augmented scale. It is a symmetrical scale used mainly for playing outside the changes. The structure of an augmented scale is thus: half-step, minor 3rd, half-step, minor 3rd, etc.

SAT

Workout #160   Drum Tracks: 16–18   Type: Pattern   Genre: Funk

Here is a common "mode" pattern applied to a C#/D augmented scale (starting on a minor 3rd).

SUN

Workout #161   Drum Tracks: 13–15   Type: Technique   Genre: Rock

In this workout, once again, we end the week with a rhythmic exercise. This time we'll be playing a 12-tone row, which is any series of all 12 chromatic notes that don't repeat each other until the sequence is completed. 12-tone harmony (or serialism), a technique invented by 20th century composer Arnold Schoenberg, was also practiced by jazz composers such as Bill Evans and Gunther Schuller.

MON

Workout #162   **Drum Tracks:** 1–3   **Type:** Technique/Lick   **Genre:** Swing

This week we'll be working on understanding tritone substitutions for the ii–V7–I chord progression. In this first example, an E7 lick is substituted for the B♭7 chord in measure 2.

TUE

Workout #163   **Drum Tracks:** 7–9   **Type:** Technique/Lick   **Genre:** Shuffle

Let's look at another example of a tritone substitution over the V7 chord, in this case, substituting a B7 lick for the F7 in measure 2. Use right side key 3 (rsk 3) for the trill fingering in measure 4.

Right Side Key 3
(C to D trill)

WED

Workout #164   **Drum Tracks:** 22, 23   **Type:** Technique/Lick   **Genre:** Bossa Nova

In jazz improvisation, any ii chord can be substituted for a V7 chord within a ii–V–I progression. This is because both of the scales used will stem from the same major scale, which is the I chord. In this substitution workout, the tritone of the ii (Am7) is substituted for the V7 in measure 2, so we end up playing E♭m7 over D7.

THU

Workout #165 **Drum Tracks:** 25 **Type:** Technique/Lick **Genre:** Reggae

This time the V7 is substituted for the ii in measure 1 (A7 for Em7), and the tritone of the V7 is substituted for the V7 in measure 2 (E♭7 for A7). It sounds complicated, but once you hear it, it will sound vaguely familiar to any bebop fan. Most notably, saxophonist Sonny Rollins and pianist Bud Powell have widely used similar licks on many of their recordings.

Note: The glissandos in measures 1 and 2 should be chromatic.

FRI

Workout #166 **Drum Tracks:** 10–12 **Type:** Technique/Lick **Genre:** 12/8

Here is another example of substituting the tritone of the ii for the V7 chord. The "C♯m7 for Gm7" tritone substitution in measures 1 and 2 works perfectly. Because we've diatonically lowered the sequence by a 3rd in measures 3 and 4, the C♯m7 chord substitution needed to be changed to a C♯ diminished scale to maintain tonality. The B♮ (7th) of the C♯ minor would have clashed with both the 7th and the root of the C dominant chord. (You probably didn't need such a pontifical analysis, but there it is.)

SAT

Workout #167 **Drum Tracks:** 27, 28 **Type:** Technique/Lick **Genre:** New Orleans 2nd Line

Here is a generic tritone substitution for the V7 chord. A C major triad is substituted for the F♯7 in measure 2.

SUN

Workout #168 **Drum Tracks:** 29 **Type:** Rhythm/Pattern **Genre:** Latin

Let's end the week with a tricky little rhythmic workout. It features descending major 2nds ascending in half steps.

SAXOPHONE AEROBICS

WEEK 25

MON

Workout #169   **Drum Tracks:** 19–21   **Type:** Lick/Pattern   **Genre:** Jazz Waltz

This week we'll be working on playing triad pairs over altered dominant chords. In this first exercise, a pattern is created using two major triads a major 2nd apart, alternating between a D triad and a C triad over a C13#11 chord.

TUE

Workout #170   **Drum Tracks:** 14, 15   **Type:** Lick Pattern   **Genre:** Rock

Today we see an A7#9 chord with A and C alternating major triad pairs, a minor 3rd apart.

WED

Workout #171   **Drum Tracks:** 23, 24   **Type:** Lick/Pattern **Genre:** Bossa Nova

Measure 1 of this workout is an arpeggio of the D altered chord. Two major triads, B♭ and A♭ (a major 2nd apart), can played over a D7#9(#5) (altered) chord. Note that neither of these triads is the root triad. They sound good, though, because an A♭ triad contains the #11, 7, and ♭9, and the B♭ triad contains the #5, tonic, and #9.

THU

Workout #172   **Drum Tracks:** 27, 28   **Type:** Lick/Pattern   **Genre:** New Orleans 2nd Line

This triad pair is the interval of a major 6th apart. The root triad, F major, can be alternated with a D major triad over an F13♭9 chord.

FRI

Workout #173   **Drum Tracks:** 30   **Type:** Lick/Pattern   **Genre:** Latin

Four different sets of major triads can be used over a dominant ♭9 chord. For a B7♭9 chord, the triads are all a minor 3rd apart: B, D, F, A♭.

SAT

Workout #174   **Drum Tracks:** 4, 5   **Type:** Technique   **Genre:** Swing

This is an exercise with minor 7ths spanning the full standard range of the saxophone. Try to keep the volume consistent throughout this exercise, and play long, legato notes.

SUN

Workout #175   **Drum Tracks:** 2, 3   **Type:** Rhythm   **Genre:** Swing

It's time for our weekly rhythm exercise. Although this notation is a bit difficult to sight read, it does conform to the engraving standards of most music publishers, and you will occasionally see these rhythms written this way.

WEEK 26

MON

Workout #176 **Drum Tracks:** 5, 6 **Type:** Pattern/Lick **Genre:** Swing

The standard tune "Lover" by Rogers and Hart has a chromatically descending ii–V chord progression on the verses ("A" sections) of the tune. "The Eternal Triangle" by saxophonist Sonny Stitt is another that uses this progression, on the bridge of the tune ("B" section). Because these tunes are both usually played at extremely fast tempos, improvisers will typically play melodic sequences over these changes using arpeggios and patterns. This exercise (transposed for alto sax) incorporates a 1-3-5-7-6 pattern in which the sixth degree of the ii chord becomes the third degree of the V chord. Also, note that the pattern is anticipated: The sequence occurs on beat 4 instead of beat 1 of the following measure.

Note: You'll find some downward runs in this exercise. Separate marked notes from their preceding notes, and start each downward run from a random high note. Listening to the recorded example will explain it far better than written words ever could.

TUE

Workout #177 **Drum Tracks:** 5, 6 **Type:** Pattern/Lick **Genre:** Swing

This is a 5-6-7-8-9 pattern, also anticipated, on measures 1 and 2. In measures 3 and 4 we see an anticipated 9-7-5-3-2-1 pattern. (Transposed for tenor sax.)

Note: The demo track is played on tenor sax.

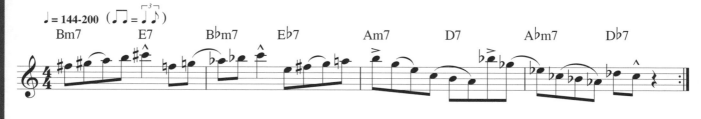

WED

Workout #178 **Drum Tracks:** 23, 24 **Type:** Pattern/Lick **Genre:** Bossa Nova

Today's etude is a longer sequence that stretches over the first two measures, and is mirrored down a whole step in measures 3 and 4. The changes have been transposed for alto sax.

Note: The demo track is played on alto sax.

THU

Workout #179   **Drum Tracks:** 8, 9   **Type:** Pattern/Lick   **Genre:** Shuffle

Here is a long sequence that is anticipated by one beat (quarter note) in the tenor sax key.

Note: The demo track is played on tenor sax.

FRI

Workout #180   **Drum Tracks:** 26   **Type:** Pattern/Lick   **Genre:** Ska

This time we're just playing slurred diatonic notes that follow the changes, covering much of the saxophones range. (Transposed for tenor sax.)

Note: The demo track is played on tenor sax.

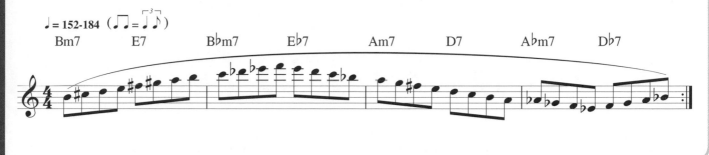

SAT

Workout #181   **Drum Tracks:** 11, 12   **Type:** Pattern/Lick/Rhythm   **Genre:** 12/8

In this exercise, we see a rarely discussed rhythm, the duplet. A duplet consists of two quarter notes played in the space of one dotted quarter note. You will see this rhythm only when the time signature is divisible by three (12/8, 9/8, 6/8, 3/8, etc.).

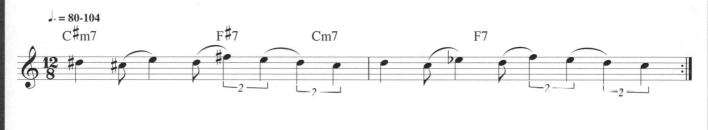

SUN

Workout #182   **Drum Tracks:** 30   **Type:** Rhythm   **Genre:** Latin

In this workout, the rhythms are notated, one wouldn't say incorrectly, but unconventionally. (Proper notation can be quite subjective). Nevertheless, you will see them written this way once in a while.

Observe the articulations: Whenever you see a sideways arrow articulation over a note head, known as a *marcato* accent in classical music, the note is to be played long, but attacked and slightly separated. A "tepee" accent, or *martellato*, means a note is to be played short and loud.

MON

Workout #183   **Drum Tracks:** 13–15   **Type:** Pattern   **Genre:** Rock

Let's begin the week with a simple four-note pattern, 1-2-5-4. It is written in descending whole steps.

TUE

Workout #184   **Drum Tracks:** 25   **Type:** Pattern   **Genre:** Reggae

Here is a descending version of the four-note pattern from the previous exercise, 5-4-1-2, written in ascending whole steps.

WED

Workout #185   **Drum Tracks:** 22, 23   **Type:** Rhythm   **Genre:** Bossa Nova

We have two more modes of the major scale to discuss. The Locrian mode, or seventh degree of a major scale, can be used over half-diminished chords. Sometimes you will see half-diminished chords written with a slash through a circle, like this: ⌀7. Here we see a B Locrian mode (ii7♭5) in measure 1 played over a B⌀7 (Bm7♭5) chord, which leads into an altered V7 chord (E7#9(#5)), and finally, into a i chord (Am7). B is the 7th degree of C major, so observe that the scale in measure 1 is a C major scale starting on a B. (The key signature also reflects this.)

THU

Workout #186 **Drum Tracks:** 2, 3 **Type:** Rhythm **Genre:** Swing

This time we see a similar ii7♭5–V–i scenario in F minor, but the half-diminished arpeggio is outlined in measure 1.

FRI

Workout #187 **Drum Tracks:** 19–21 **Type:** Rhythm **Genre:** Jazz Waltz

The Phrygian mode (third degree of a major scale) is the last mode of the major scale that we haven't discussed. It is the scale spanning measures 3-4 of this exercise. It has a Spanish sound to it. These chord changes are based on "Malagueña," by Cuban composer Ernesto Lecuona.

SAT

Workout #188 **Drum Tracks:** 26 **Type:** Rhythm **Genre:** Ska

Today we again encounter the Phrygian mode in a minor setting.

SUN

Workout #189 **Drum Tracks:** 17–18 **Type:** Rhythm **Genre:** Funk

Have fun with your funky rhythm exercise for the day. Any unmarked notes should be played legato.

WEEK 28

MON

Workout #190   **Drum Tracks:** 1–3   **Type:** Scale/Lick   **Genre:** Swing

Now it's time for us to get more familiar with the melodic minor scale. This week, every exercise will incorporate the ascending version of the melodic minor scale, so your ear can get used to its harmony. This first exercise states a G melodic minor scale verbatim in the first measure, then transforms in an effort to acclimate your ear to its tonality as the exercise continues. (Note the lack of key signatures; melodic minor scales are not derived from major scales, so conventional key signatures do not apply.)

TUE

Workout #191   **Drum Tracks:** 25   **Type:** Scale/Lick   **Genre:** Reggae

Here, an ascending arpeggio of the C melodic minor chord, Cm(maj7), morphs into a bebop lick and ends with a descending arpeggio.

WED

Workout #192   **Drum Tracks:** 22, 23   **Type:** Patttern   **Genre:** Bossa Nova

In measures 1 and 2, we see ascending diatonic 3rds in an up-up pattern. Measures 3 and 4 are descending 3rds in a down-down pattern. Observe the deceptive phrasing. Learn the pattern first and the articulations afterward.

THU

Workout #193   **Drum Tracks:** 27, 28   **Type:** Lick   **Genre:** New Orleans 2nd Line

This time, a B♭ melodic minor scale continues into a 9-7-5-1 descending arpeggio, and trails off into a bebop lick ending on the sixth, à la trumpeter Dizzy Gillespie.

FRI

Workout #194   **Drum Tracks:** 16–18   **Type:** Pattern   **Genre:** Funk

The 7, 5, 3, and 1 (tonic) of the C melodic minor chord dip down to lead tones and back in this funk exercise.
Note: Use the "one and one" fingering for the A♯ in measure 1. (Add the F key in the left hand to the fingering for B.)

SAT

Workout #195   **Drum Tracks:** 7–9   **Type:** Lick   **Genre:** Shuffle

Today's extended G melodic minor bebop lick ends with a resolving 3-5-7-9 V chord cadence.
Note: Use the bis key fingering for the B♭ on beat 1 of measure 3, and add the right side key 2 (rsk 2) to play up to the C.

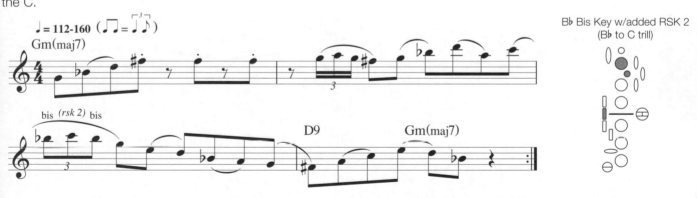

SUN

Workout #196   **Drum Tracks:** 29   **Type:** Rhythm   **Genre:** Latin

This week-ending F melodic minor rhythm workout is notated in symmetrical groups, making it somewhat difficult to decipher an otherwise "normal" rhythm.

MON

Workout #197   **Drum Tracks:** 1–3   **Type:** Pattern   **Genre:** Swing

This week we'll continue our study of the melodic minor scale. Measures 1 and 2 of this exercise are ascending G melodic minor arpeggios in an ascending up-up pattern. Measures 3 and 4 are descending arpeggios in an ascending down-down pattern.

TUE

Workout #198   **Drum Tracks:** 7–9   **Type:** Pattern   **Genre:** Shuffle

These are ascending and descending arpeggios in E♭ melodic minor, proceeding in a down-up pattern throughout the exercise.

WED

Workout #199   **Drum Tracks:** 27, 28   **Type:** Lick   **Genre:** New Orleans 2nd Line

Much of modern jazz is eclectic, in that it is influenced by many different musical styles. In this workout, melodic minor harmony is incongruously heard in a traditional jazz format.

Workout #200 **Drum Tracks:** 26 **Type:** Pattern **Genre:** Ska

The bebop melodic minor scale (the last of the four bebop scales, which we discussed in Week 17) is like a bebop major scale with a minor 3rd: The chromatic passing tone, a defining trait of all bebop scales, occurs between the fifth and the sixth degrees of the melodic minor scale.

Workout #201 **Drum Tracks:** 10–12 **Type:** Pattern **Genre:** 12/8

Here is a 1-3-5-7-9 arpeggio pattern that ends with a modification of probably the most common phrase in bebop, the "Cry Me River" lick (an indirect quote from the melody of the song of the same name by Arthur Hamilton), 9-8-5-♭3-2-1. You'll hear variations on this motif in countless recorded bebop solos.

Workout #202 **Drum Tracks:** 22, 23 **Type:** Lick **Genre:** Bossa Nova

This bebop lick in D melodic minor incorporates several articulations and techniques we've covered so far. Use lip falls instead of note glissandos (drop jaw).

Workout #203 **Drum Tracks:** 13–15 **Type:** Rhythm **Genre:** Rock

Play these displaced triplets legato throughout this B♭ melodic minor exercise.
Hint: Always be aware of beats 1 and 4.

MON

Workout #204   **Drum Tracks:** 4, 5   **Type:** Scale   **Genre:** Swing

For the next three weeks, we'll be studying the modes of the melodic minor scale. We'll begin with the second degree of the melodic minor scale, which is a suspended ♭9 scale (7sus♭9). In this exercise, the "sus ♭9" scale is played straight up and down in measures 1 and 2. Measures 3 and 4 show a modified arpeggio highlighting the ♭9/♭2 (1, ♭2, 4, 5, 8, 5, 4, ♭2, 1).

TUE

Workout #205   **Drum Tracks:** 22–24   **Type:** Pattern   **Genre:** Bossa Nova

Ascending diatonic 3rds of the G suspended ♭9 scale in an up-up pattern start off this exercise, which ends with descending diatonic 3rds in a down-down pattern.

WED

Workout #206   **Drum Tracks:** 19-21   **Type:** Pattern   **Genre:** Jazz Waltz

This progression demonstrates a common usage of the suspended ♭9 scale: resolving a sus9 chord. Measures 1 and 2 outline a sus9 chord (Bm7/E), and measures 3 and 4 outline a sus♭9 chord (Bm7♭5/E), which would ultimately resolve to some kind of A major chord.

THU

Workout #207 **Drum Tracks:** 25 **Type:** Scale **Genre:** Reggae

The third degree of a melodic minor scale is the Lydian augmented scale (notated as maj7#5). Here is a E♭ Lydian augmented scale and arpeggio. In jazz, this chord is often written as G/E♭.

Note: This scale has also been called the whole-tone-diminished scale, which can be a bit confusing, because there is also a diminished-whole-tone scale (the altered scale, coming up in Week 32). Anyway, we're going to use Lydian augmented.

♩ = 100-136
E♭maj7#5

FRI

Workout #208 **Drum Tracks:** 16–18 **Type:** Pattern **Genre:** Funk

Here we have diatonic triads of an A♭ Lydian augmented scale ascending in an up-down pattern. This chord might also be written as C/A♭.

Note: One could think of a Lydian augmented chord as a tonic with a major triad starting on the major 3rd above the tonic.

♩ = 60-84
A♭maj7#5

SAT

Workout #209 **Drum Tracks:** 30 **Type:** Pattern **Genre:** Latin

This time we'll alternate an F augmented triad and a G major triad (F+/G) to show another way to use triads in Lydian augmented harmony.

♩ = 126-168
Fmaj7#5

SUN

Workout #210 **Drum Tracks:** 6 **Type:** Rhythm **Genre:** Fast Swing

Okay, this rhythmic workout is supposed to be played at a fast tempo. It works the extremities of the saxophone's normal range. The rhythm was inspired by the introduction to a tune by tenor saxophonist Wayne Shorter, "The Soothsayer."

♩ = 220-280
N.C.

MON

Workout #211   **Drum Tracks:** 22, 23   **Type:** Scale/Lick   **Genre:** Bossa Nova

In improvisation, the most commonly used mode of the melodic minor scale is probably the Lydian dominant scale, which starts on the fourth degree of a melodic minor scale. This scale has been exploited by composers and musicians since the art form known as jazz was in its earliest stages of development. Here is a complicated F7#11 arpeggio pattern (we'll just call it a lick) that is kicked off with an ascending Lydian dominant scale.

TUE

Workout #212   **Drum Tracks:** 19, 20   **Type:** Pattern/Lick   **Genre:** Jazz Waltz

Today we'll be playing a B♭ Lydian dominant arpeggio that trails off into a multi-pattern lick.

Hint: For these turns, make sure to play triplets that go up to the next diatonic (within the scale) note and back to the original note before continuing on to the next note. Use the B♭ bis key and add rsk 2 for the turn in measure 2.

WED

Workout #213   **Drum Tracks:** 11–12   **Type:** Pattern/Lick   **Genre:** 12/8

Let's practice another pattern-based G Lydian dominant lick.

THU

Workout #214   **Drum Tracks:** 16, 17   **Type:** Lick   **Genre:** Funk

The fifth degree of the melodic minor scale is a dominant ♭6 scale. Here we have a funk lick in G dominant ♭6 that starts off with a G7♭6 arpeggio.

FRI

Workout #215   **Drum Tracks:** 7, 8   **Type:** Pattern/Lick   **Genre:** Shuffle

You should be able to play this exercise slowly before attempting to play it fast. Yes, the notes may be easy for you to play, but the phrasing might be a bit of a challenge.

SAT

Workout #216   **Drum Tracks:** 26   **Type:** Pattern   **Genre:** Ska

Here is an A dominant ♭6 arpeggio exercise. It should help you to recognize the sound of this rarely used melodic minor mode.

SUN

Workout #217   **Drum Tracks:** 13, 14   **Type:** Rhythm   **Genre:** Rock

Quintuplets are the subject of this rhythm workout in E♭ major.

Hint: To get started with the feel of these non-traditional rhythms, you can think of them as an eighth-note triplet grouped together with two eighth notes. Once you can do that, you can begin to even out the quintuplets' divisions.

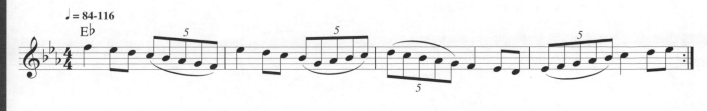

MON

Workout #218   **Drum Tracks:** 30   **Type:** Scale/Lick   **Genre:** Latin

The sixth degree of the melodic minor scale is an important mode in jazz, the half-diminished scale. It is similar to the Locrian mode of the major scale, but the Locrian mode has a ♭2. The half-diminished scale will work better most of the time when you see a m7♭5 (or ∅7) chord symbol. In this exercise, we see an ascending Am7♭5 scale and lick that resolves to a Dsus♭9, which also resolves to a V♭9 (D7♭9).

TUE

Workout #219   **Drum Tracks:** 27, 28   **Type:** Pattern/Lick   **Genre:** New Orleans 2nd Line

Try your hand at this D half-diminished (D∅7) lick. It uses patterns and scalar movement.

WED

Workout #220   **Drum Tracks:** 4, 5   **Type:** Pattern/Lick   **Genre:** Swing

Wednesday's exercise is another pattern-based lick in the key of B half-diminished.

THU

Workout #221   Drum Tracks: 7–9   Type: Scale   Genre: Shuffle

Now we've come to the final mode of the melodic minor scale, the altered scale, also known as the super-Locrian or diminished whole tone scale. For our purposes, let's keep it simple, and call it the altered scale, since it's mainly used over altered chords (V#9). In this exercise, we state the B altered scale up to the ninth and back down in measure 1 and 2, and end with a 1-3-5-7-9 (B7#9(#5)) arpeggio.

FRI

Workout #222   Drum Tracks: 20, 21   Type: Lick   Genre: Jazz Waltz

When you see an E7#9(#5) during improvisation, think: F melodic minor scale starting on E. It will become easier for you to think about chord symbols like this the more you practice this technique. To demonstrate this type of analysis, measure 1 of this lick starts with an E (the tonic), followed by an F melodic minor ascending arpeggio.

SAT

Workout #223   Drum Tracks: 29   Type: Pattern   Genre: Latin

Each measure of this exercise shows a different pattern of diatonic thirds of the C# altered scale: 1) ascending up-up; 2) ascending down-down; 3) descending down-up; 4) descending up-down.

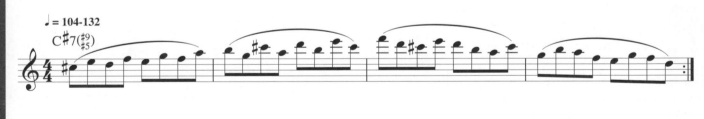

SUN

Workout #224   Drum Tracks: 25   Type: Rhythm   Genre: Reggae

Note the symmetrical rhythm pattern in this E major exercise. Rhythms will become increasingly asymmetrical and the melodies increasingly atonal as we proceed. Observe that the intervals between the notes in this workout increase incrementally and diatonically.

MON

Workout #225   **Drum Tracks:** 1, 4   **Type:** Technique   **Genre:** Swing

Everybody knows that the way we attack a note is very important. We've been correctly taught to exaggerate articulations and dynamics (which we'll be discussing further next week). A mature musician also knows that it is just as important to end a held note properly, and to know where to release it. There doesn't always seem to be a general consensus as to where exactly to release notes, but there are some unwritten, common sense rules:

1. Hold the note as long as possible. For half notes and whole notes, we usually hold the note until the following downbeat. If one of these notes is a dotted-quarter note, or tied to an eighth note (or a note of lesser value), the composer or arranger has written in the cutoff. In this case, you are expected to cut off at the end of the extended note.
2. Leave space where space is written. Release the note in time to leave the space that the composer/arranger has specified.
3. Leave room to breathe. There are usually logical breathing points in music (rests), but if you hold a note too long, you may miss your chance to take a breath.

In this A major exercise, the cutoff points are written in for you. For example, when you see -3 (measure 1) you should release the note right on beat 3, and no further.

TUE

Workout #226   **Drum Tracks:** 13, 14   **Type:** Technique   **Genre:** Rock

Here, once again, cutoffs are written in for you. (Key of E♭ major).

WED

Workout #227   **Drum Tracks:** 22   **Type:** Technique   **Genre:** Bossa Nova

In this E major exercise, there is no cutoff written for the held note in measure 3. Leave space where space is written.

THU

Workout #228   **Drum Tracks:** 25   **Type:** Technique   **Genre:** Reggae

This A♭ cutoff exercise has no written cutoffs. Remember to release held notes on the downbeat following the held note.

FRI

Workout #229   **Drum Tracks:** 7   **Type:** Technique   **Genre:** Shuffle

This is another cutoff exercise in G♯ minor. Follow all the "common sense" rules mentioned in Workout #225.

SAT

Workout #230   **Drum Tracks:** 29   **Type:** Technique   **Genre:** Latin

If a composer or arranger has written a held note with its cutoff on a specific note division, you are expected to cut off the note after holding it to its full value. For example, in measure 2, you are supposed to cut off the dotted-quarter note no further than the "and" of beat 4.

Note: Many horn sections have their own ideas of where notes should be cut off. You should probably just follow the lead trumpet player.

SUN

Workout #231   **Drum Tracks:** 16   **Type:** Rhythm   **Genre:** Funk

This week's rhythm exercise includes some 32nd notes. No worries. The tempo is slow enough that you should be able to hear the subdivisions of each beat.

MON

Workout #232   **Drum Tracks:** 8   **Type:** Technique   **Genre:** Shuffle

Dynamics will be our main topic this week. In jazz and popular music, if the composer has gone to the trouble of writing in dynamics, they are meant to be exaggerated. In this first workout we see crescendos, diminuendos, and volume expressions like *piano* (softly) and *forte* (loudly). Exaggerate them all in this G major exercise. Measures 3 and 4 don't have a written *forte*, so you will need to apply exaggeration. Also, don't forget to cut off notes in their proper place.

TUE

Workout #233   **Drum Tracks:** 14   **Type:** Technique   **Genre:** Rock

This workout in F major includes more extreme dynamics, *pianissimo* (very softly) and *fortissimo* (very loudly). There's also a *forte piano* (***fp***), which means attack the note loudly and diminish to soft immediately. By measure 4, it is implied (through exaggeration) that you should be back up to a *fortissimo* volume before the final diminuendo.

WED

Workout #234   **Drum Tracks:** 19, 20   **Type:** Technique   **Genre:** Jazz Waltz

Follow the dynamics in this C major exercise. There is a ***p*** *sub.* at the end of measure 2. *Subito* means suddenly, so at that point you should immediately play softly.

THU

Workout #235   **Drum Tracks:** 11, 12   **Type:** Technique   **Genre:** 12/8

Delineate the *pianissimo* and *fortissimo* phrases in this example of dynamic contrast. It's in the key of F♯ major.

FRI

Workout #236   **Drum Tracks:** 24   **Type:** Technique   **Genre:** Bossa Nova

Measures 1 and 2 of this exercise have ***fp*** attacks with crescendos. Measures 3 and 4 have ***f*** attacks with diminuendos. Remember to cutoff notes in time to leave space.

Note: It would have made no sense to write ***fp*** before the diminuendos in measures 3 and 4, because after the instant diminuendo, there would be nowhere to diminuendo.

SAT

Workout #237   **Drum Tracks:** 16, 17   **Type:** Technique   **Genre:** Funk

Follow the overabundance of dynamics in this B minor funk horn line. You should be able to tell a marked difference in volume between the ***mp*** in measure 1 and the ***mf*** in measure 3. (Exaggerate dynamics!)

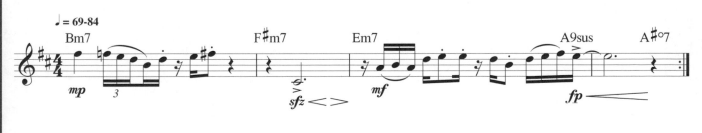

SUN

Workout #238   **Drum Tracks:** 26   **Type:** Rhythm   **Genre:** Ska

Enjoy your weekly rhythm workout. It includes dynamics, of course.

MON

Workout #239   **Drum Tracks:** 1–3   **Type:** Technique   **Genre:** Swing

There is a whole range above the "normal" range of the saxophone called the altissimo range. It is possible to play scales and lines in the altissimo on all saxophones. Fingerings will differ on a few notes between saxes, even between saxes of the same range and brand. Play these next six exercises as slowly as necessary, and gradually speed them up. This chromatic workout includes the first altissimo note: high G. Stick to the routine and learn one altissimo fingering per day.

Note: On the demo track, the alto plays first, followed by the tenor.

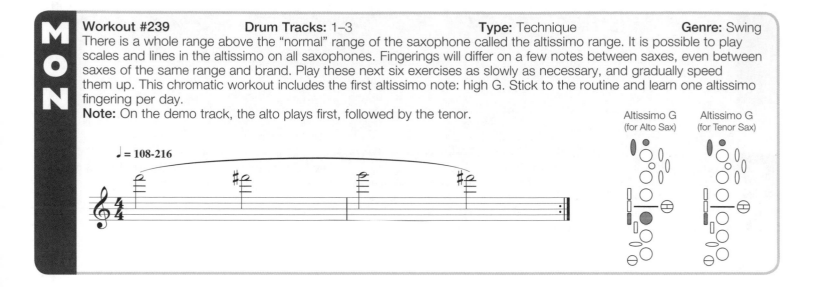

Altissimo G (for Alto Sax)   Altissimo G (for Tenor Sax)

TUE

Workout #240   **Drum Tracks:** 1–3   **Type:** Technique   **Genre:** Swing

The altissimo G#/A♭ occurs on beat 3 of measure 1 in this triad workout.

Note: On the demo track, the alto plays first, followed by the tenor.

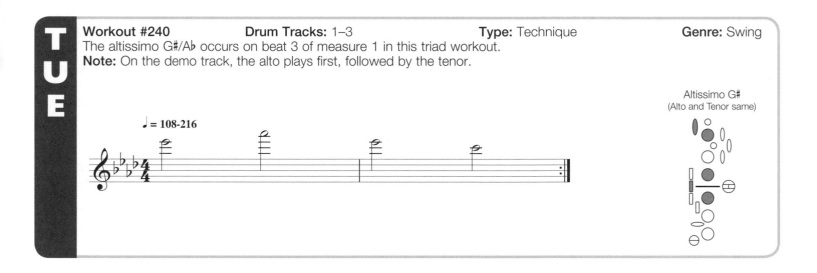

Altissimo G# (Alto and Tenor same)

WED

Workout #241   **Drum Tracks:** 1–3   **Type:** Technique   **Genre:** Swing

Practice this A major triad that incorporates altissimo A (beat 3 of measure 1).

Note: On the demo track, the alto plays first, followed by the tenor.

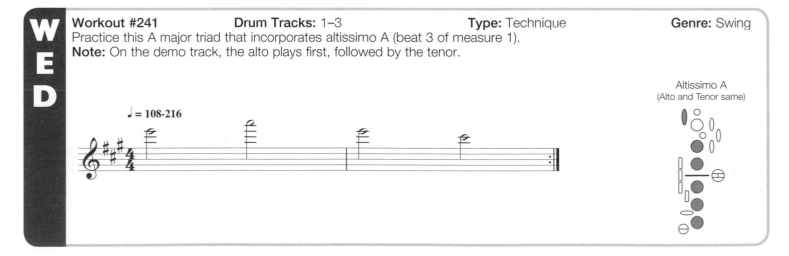

Altissimo A (Alto and Tenor same)

THU

Workout #242 **Drum Tracks:** 1–3 **Type:** Technique **Genre:** Swing

Five ledger lines is too many to read (you'll never see notes written that high), so at this point, we'll start reading down an octave with the *8va* (octave) symbol. Here's altissimo A#/B♭ on beat 1 of measure 2.

Note: On the demo track, the alto plays first, followed by the tenor.

Altissimo A#/B♭
(Alto and Tenor same)

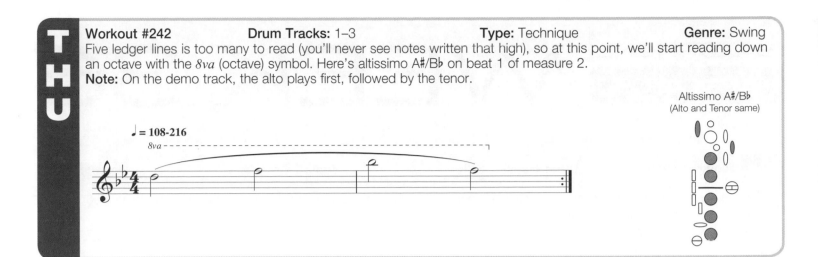

FRI

Workout #243 **Drum Tracks:** 1–3 **Type:** Technique **Genre:** Swing

Altissimo B makes an appearance on beat 3 of measure 1 in this B major triad workout.

Note: On the demo track, the alto plays first, followed by the tenor.

Altissimo B
(Alto and Tenor same)

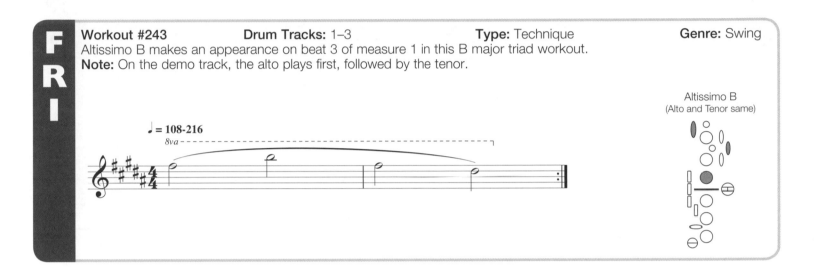

SAT

Workout #244 **Drum Tracks:** 1–3 **Type:** Technique **Genre:** Swing

Altissimo C is at the beginning of measure 2 in this C major triad exercise.

Note: On the demo track, the alto plays first, followed by the tenor.

Altissimo C
(Alto and Tenor same)

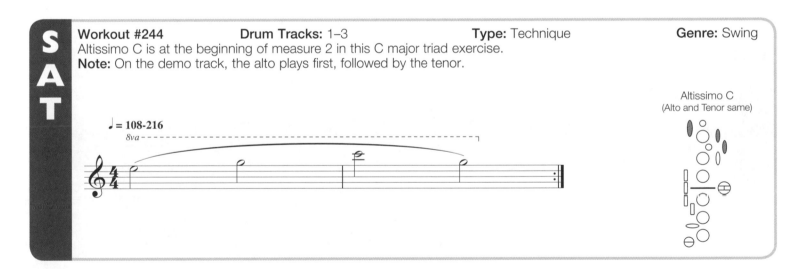

SUN

Workout #245 **Drum Tracks:** 19, 20 **Type:** Rhythm **Genre:** Jazz Waltz

Here is a sight-reading/rhythm exercise with odd chord changes and an improvisatory feel.

Note: The demo track is played on alto sax.

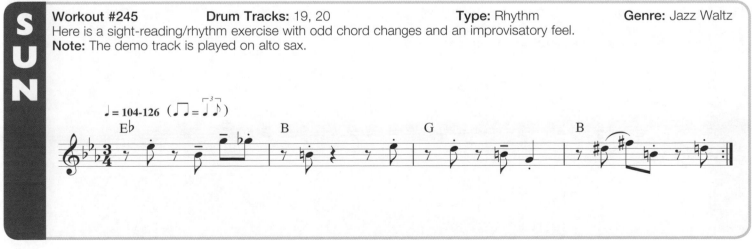

MON

Workout #246   **Drum Tracks:** 16–18   **Type:** Technique   **Genre:** Funk

This week we'll start playing scales and patterns in the altissimo range. Take it slowly, as indicated. If you go too fast, you will get frustrated. In this first exercise, always be looking ahead to the next note, and imagine fingering that note as you hold your current note.

Note: The demo track is played on alto sax.

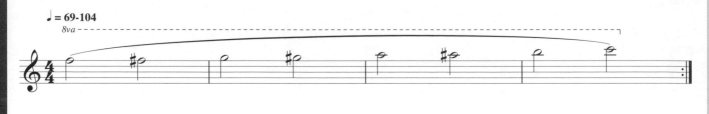

TUE

Workout #247   **Drum Tracks:** 16–18   **Type:** Technique   **Genre:** Funk

It is a good idea to start practicing scales and patterns as high as you want to be able to play. In this book, we stop at double-high C. If you feel like it, you can play much higher than that. For example, Lenny Pickett, saxophonist from the *Saturday Night Live* band, regularly plays an octave above double-high D on tenor sax. Before him, Junior Walker was manipulating the altissimo of the tenor sax, and before Junior, Earl Bostic was doing it on alto sax. Check out all three of these players for R&B sax inspiration. Here is a chromatic altissimo exercise.

Note: The demo track is played on tenor sax.

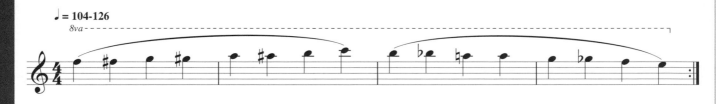

WED

Workout #248   **Drum Tracks:** 16–18   **Type:** Technique   **Genre:** Funk

Note the tenuto marks in this chromatic triad exercise for the altissimo range.

Note: The demo track is played on alto sax.

THU

Workout #249 **Drum Tracks:** 16–18 **Type:** Technique **Genre:** Funk

These are major 1-2-3-1 patterns in the altissimo. Give special attention to the articulation.

Note: The demo track is played on tenor sax.

FRI

Workout #250 **Drum Tracks:** 16–18 **Type:** Technique **Genre:** Funk

Measures 1 and 2 of this altissimo workout are an excerpt from the E major scale, and measures 3 and 4 are an excerpt from the F major scale.

Note: The demo track is played on alto sax.

SAT

Workout #251 **Drum Tracks:** 16–18 **Type:** Technique **Genre:** Funk

Don't forget to observe the phrasing in this chromatic up-down 1-2-3-5 exercise.

Note: The demo track is played on tenor sax.

SUN

Workout #252 **Drum Tracks:** 7–9 **Type:** Rhythm **Genre:** Shuffle

This week's rhythm workout includes some altissimo notes and stretches across three octaves.

Note: The demo track is played on alto sax.

M O N

Workout #253   **Drum Tracks:** 10–12   **Type:** Technique   **Genre:** Funk

Every note on any acoustic instrument is a combination of wave frequencies called harmonic partials. The lowest partial of the series is called the fundamental, and every other note in the same series is called an overtone. Each one of these overtones can be singled out and controlled on the saxophone. This week we will begin learning the most useful section of the overtone series. Once you can play these exercises, not only will your sound improve, but you will also have learned several false fingerings. This first exercise displays the overtone series for low B♭.

Notes: Regarding the notation, you will use the fingering for the fundamental throughout this exercise (in parentheses), but sound the overtones above them. They occur in order of their appearance in the overtone series. Do not use the octave key. Try to play each partial as much in tune as possible.

Tongue the fundamental, but don't tongue the upper partials in this exercise – use breath articulation only. (In other words, say hoo-hoo instead of tah-tah.)

Hint: If you have trouble hearing which partial you are supposed to be sounding, test it by playing its "true" fingering (down an octave if necessary).

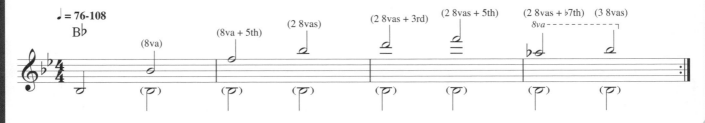

T U E

Workout #254   **Drum Tracks:** 10–12   **Type:** Technique   **Genre:** Funk

This is the overtone series for low B. As in the previous exercise, attack notes using only breath articulations.

Note: The last two partials may be flat, because of the physics of each individual instrument. (Some saxes are more in tune than others.) If these notes are flat, you will just have to live with this discord, or deal with it by lipping down from a higher partial (which sounds much easier than it is).

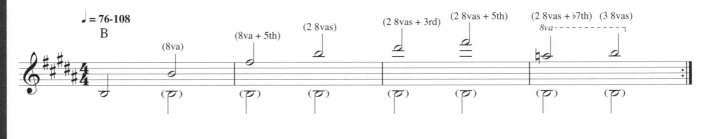

W E D

Workout #255   **Drum Tracks:** 13   **Type:** Technique   **Genre:** Funk

Now let's use the overtone series for low C. To explain what you should be hearing, the order of notes will be as such: fundamental, octave, fundamental, octave + fifth, etc.

Note: It required several takes before I was satisfied with the recorded demonstration of this exercise, and it is not perfect. The purpose of this workout is laryngeal flexibility, not intonation. (I had to lip the last two overtones down from higher partials, because those notes are extremely flat.) Don't worry about getting those last two partials perfectly in tune, or you'll go insane. They simply will not be in tune, so try and find a way to make it work and move on.

Workout #256   **Drum Tracks:** 13, 14   **Type:** Technique   **Genre:** Rock

Finger the bottom notes and sound the top notes, without using the octave key. The interval is two octaves. Some notes will be out of tune. (It's not you, it's the instrument.) Just do the best you can with the intonation.

Note: The D will be a half-step flat on all saxes, that's why we're using the fingering for palm D in this exercise (without the octave key, of course).

Workout #257   **Drum Tracks:** 10–12   **Type:** Technique   **Genre:** Funk

Finger the bottom notes and sound the top notes an octave and a 5th above. This time, you can use the octave key. These are all useful false fingerings. If you never knew any false fingerings before, now you know *nine* of them. They are usually indicated by a "+" over the note.

Note: Use the octave key throughout.

Workout #258   **Drum Tracks:** 10–12   **Type:** Technique   **Genre:** Funk

This time we'll be alternating between the "true" fingerings and "false" fingerings. This is also a useful improvisational technique used extensively by John Coltrane in the early 1960s on tunes like "Chasin' the Trane."

Note: Substitute the low C# key for the G# key when playing G# throughout this exercise. It will sound the same, but jumping to the fingering for low C# will be much easier. Use the octave key throughout.

G# alternate fingering

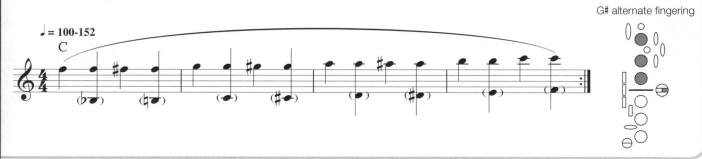

Workout #259   **Drum Tracks:** 1–3   **Type:** Rhythm   **Genre:** Swing

We'll end the week with a mildly atonal rhythmic exercise.

WEEK 38

MON

Workout #260   **Drum Tracks:** 4, 5   **Type:** Technique   **Genre:** Swing

After last week's overtone workouts, we're ready to tackle some false fingering exercises. Employing the octave key, use the fingering for an octave and a perfect 5th below each note with a "+" above it. For example, when you see a G with a plus sign, finger a low C with the octave key for the false fingering. This week's first exercise is a 1-2-3-1 pattern with an alternating true-false fingering pattern. Try to match the sound of the false and true fingerings as closely as possible.

TUE

Workout #261   **Drum Tracks:** 4, 5   **Type:** Technique   **Genre:** Swing

Here's a chromatically descending true-false pattern.

WED

Workout #262   **Drum Tracks:** 10–12   **Type:** Technique   **Genre:** 12/8

This exercise is also a chromatically descending "4-5-false 5" pattern.

Workout #263 **Drum Tracks:** 4 **Type:** Technique **Genre:** Swing

Today's workout is a chromatically descending "5-false 5-4-5" pattern.

♩ = 88-104

Workout #264 **Drum Tracks:** 4, 5 **Type:** Technique **Genre:** Swing

This is a practical usage of false fingerings, based on the work of John Coltrane. Coltrane played a lot of 5th-based false fingerings in his solos from the early 1960s, which had a huge influence on younger players like David Liebman, Steve Grossman, and Michael Brecker.

♩ = 80-112

Workout #265 **Drum Tracks:** 22–24 **Type:** Technique **Genre:** Bossa Nova

Let's try an alternating "true-false, false-true" pattern. This workout is difficult to master. Working to match the sounds of false and true fingerings may be a step to helping you achieve your own voice on your instrument.

♩ = 100-144

Workout #266 **Drum Tracks:** 30 **Type:** Rhythm **Genre:** Latin

This rhythm workout further demonstrates how unconventional notation can often be somewhat difficult to read. The quarter notes in the middle of each of these measures make sense rhythmically, but this exercise would be much easier to read if each measure were split down the middle, with two eighth notes tied together instead. Recognizing tricky rhythms and odd notation will help prepare you for sight reading.

♩ = 132-168

WEEK 39

MON

Workout #267 **Drum Tracks:** 27, 28 **Type:** Technique **Genre:** New Orleans 2nd Line

This week we'll explore some novel and practical ways to use false fingerings. Saxophonists of the 1930s, most notably Lester Young, combined false fingerings and rhythmic patterns to produce some startling effects. These ideas were used and modified by younger players like Sonny Stitt and Dexter Gordon. This short etude should help you gain an understanding of how to create rhythmic patterns with false fingerings.

Note: New fingering: Palm D without the octave key, which is a false fingering for middle D. This alternate fingering was used regularly by jazz saxophonists Lester Young, Charlie Parker, and Dexter Gordon, among many others.

Palm D
(false fingering)

TUE

Workout #268 **Drum Tracks:** 22–24 **Type:** Technique **Genre:** Bossa Nova

Today's rhythmic false fingerings workout features eighth notes in groups of three.

WED

Workout #269 **Drum Tracks:** 13, 14 **Type:** Technique **Genre:** Rock

These minor 1-2-3-5 patterns combine groups of notes with false fingerings and groups with regular notes. John Coltrane heavily exploited this technique in the 1960s.

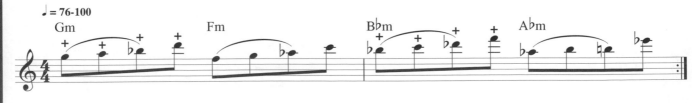

THU

Workout #270 **Drum Tracks:** 1, 2 **Type:** Technique **Genre:** Swing

Eventually, Coltrane integrated false fingerings into his playing so much that they almost became unnoticeable. He did so much innovating that some of his techniques have yet to be deciphered, or at the very least, haven't been discussed outside of private lessons with Coltrane's direct disciples. We're getting into some undiscovered territory, exploring new ways to combine false fingerings and true fingerings. Coltrane was doing this kind of thing back in the 1960s, and there still aren't many exercises with which to practice false fingerings, but here's one.

FRI

Workout #271 **Drum Tracks:** 4–6 **Type:** Technique **Genre:** Swing

This lick, presented in four different keys, is based on those used by bebop saxophonists in the 1950s. When you see a note with a "+" over it in this exercise, use the fingering for the note one octave below that note.

Note: Use the octave key starting with the false fingering in each one-measure phrase.

SAT

Workout #272 **Drum Tracks:** 25 **Type:** Technique **Genre:** Reggae

Here is a scale in which the false fingerings and true fingerings alternate in groups of two. False fingerings in this exercise will all be a perfect 5th below the written note.

SUN

Workout #273 **Drum Tracks:** 7, 8 **Type:** Rhythm/Technique **Genre:** Shuffle

Have fun with your weekly rhythmic workout. It incorporates some false fingerings in half steps.

MON

Workout #274   **Drum Tracks:** 22–24   **Type:** Technique   **Genre:** Bossa Nova

Half-tonguing is an advanced phrasing technique that is used to create a "ghosted" or muted effect on the saxophone. Half-tonguing is done by laying the tip of your tongue on the reed just enough that the reed will still vibrate, albeit with a muted sound. In this first half-tonguing exercise, mute the notes with an *h.t.* above them. Note that the unmuted notes will be much louder.

TUE

Workout #275   **Drum Tracks:** 4–6   **Type:** Technique   **Genre:** Swing

In this chromatic exercise, the half-tongued notes occur after the unmuted notes at a much faster tempo.

WED

Workout #276   **Drum Tracks:** 13–15   **Type:** Technique   **Genre:** Funk

In the G major scale that follows, every other note is half-tongued.

THU

Workout #277   **Drum Tracks:** 4–6   **Type:** Technique   **Genre:** Swing

Half-tonguing can be used along with false fingering for a effect. This exercise is inspired by the innovations of tenor saxophonists Eddie "Lockjaw" Davis and Sonny Stitt. As usual, a "+" over a note stands for "use a false fingering." Because some of the slurs end up looking like ties in this workout, I've differentiated them by placing an "o" over regular notes, which means "use the traditional fingering."

FRI

Workout #278   **Drum Tracks:** 27–28   **Type:** Rhythm   **Genre:** New Orleans 2nd Line

This chromatic exercise demonstrates a syncopated use of half-tonguing.

SAT

Workout #279   **Drum Tracks:** 1–3   **Type:** Technique   **Genre:** Swing

Alto saxophonist Cannonball Adderley used half-tonguing to mute several notes of a phrase so that when he unmuted the notes, they would pop explosively out of his melodic lines. This workout has the half-tonguing and phrasing written the way he might have played it.

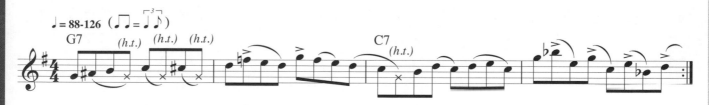

SUN

Workout #280   **Drum Tracks:** 29   **Type:** Rhythm/Technique   **Genre:** Latin

Here is a rhythm exercise that includes quintuplets and half-tonguing techniques. Make sure you can hear a difference between the quintuplet in measure 1 and the triplet plus two eighth notes in measure 2. The quintuplet should have five equal beat divisions. (We'll discuss tuplets in depth during Week 43.)

WEEK 41

MON

Workout #281 **Drum Tracks:** 1, 2 **Type:** Technique **Genre:** Swing

This week we'll be examining the triplet feel, an essential concept in the genre of swing music. Swing will often be noted in the time signature. The rhythm section keeps a consistent triplet feel in straight-ahead combo settings, so it is not necessary for a soloist to swing notes constantly. Sometimes it is much more swinging to play straight eighths over a rhythm section playing triplet feel. Nevertheless, it is important to know the difference between swing and straight feel. In this exercise, the triplet feel is written literally in measure 1; in measure 2, it is implied. Legato tongue every note.

TUE

Workout #282 **Drum Tracks:** 1, 2 **Type:** Technique **Genre:** Swing

For this workout, you will need to use the drum tracks. Play the first two measures as written, with triplet feel. Play the last two measures straight. The melody and the phrase markings are exactly the same in both instances.
Note: Many great jazz saxophonists, often play straight eighths over swing, even on ballads. (The late Dexter Gordon was especially noted for this.) They can achieve a swing feel using phrasing (back-tonguing, etc.) instead of strictly playing triplet feel. Also, sometimes it just sounds really cool to play straight over swing.

WED

Workout #283 **Drum Tracks:** 22, 23 **Type:** Technique **Genre:** Bossa Nova

You will need the drum tracks for this exercise, too. Over a straight-eighths groove, swing the eighth notes in measures 3 and 4. Legato tongue every note.

THU

Workout #284   **Drum Tracks:** 4   **Type:** Technique   **Genre:** Swing

It is humanly impossible to swing 16th notes at high speed. Computers are capable of achieving this effect, and it sounds absolutely ludicrous. 16th notes are meant to be played straight in the swing genre. Here is an example of how phrasing can make 16th-note passages swing hard, even without triplet feel.

Note: In this exercise (and in general), incorporate the implied *line dynamics*. When playing in the jazz genre, there should be a subtle crescendo on ascending lines and a diminuendo on descending lines. The highest notes of a musical phrase should be accented.

FRI

Workout #285   **Drum Tracks:** 4–6   **Type:** Technique   **Genre:** Swing

In the early 1960s, trumpeter Miles Davis often ended songs with a repeated coda that used the chord progression ii–V–iii–VI. Miles's sax player from that era was George Coleman, and he was an absolute master of this progression. This workout is reminiscent of the sequenced lines he played over this coda section. Play straight eighths with the written phrasing.

Note: Apply the implied line dynamics.

SAT

Workout #286   **Drum Tracks:** 7–9   **Type:** Technique   **Genre:** Shuffle

As in the previous exercise, this is the ii–V–iii–VI progression with lines in the style of George Coleman. Legato tongue and swing the first two measures, and phrase the last two measures as written, played straight (without swing). Notice that, because of the phrasing, the last two measures will sound almost as "swinging" as the first two, even without the triplet feel.

Note: Apply line dynamics during this workout, too. They are often subtle, but now that you've learned how to use them, you'll start noticing that they occur in all types of music.

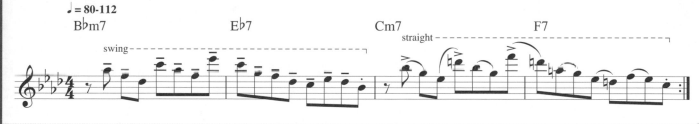

SUN

Workout #287   **Drum Tracks:** 22–24   **Type:** Rhythm   **Genre:** Bossa Nova

This oddly melodic rhythm workout includes some tricky triplet usage.

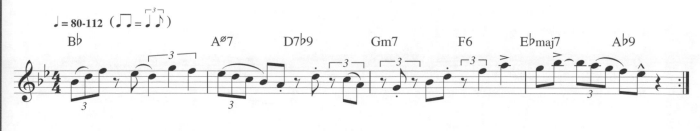

MON

Workout #288 **Drum Tracks:** 1–3 **Type:** Rhythm **Genre:** Swing

For the next two weeks, we're going to study a few polyrhythms. These are techniques usually practiced by percussionists, but some saxophonists, most notably Joe Henderson, have also conquered this technique. This exercise in G Dorian is one of the simpler examples of polyrhythm: triplets in groups of four notes.

TUE

Workout #289 **Drum Tracks:** 16–18 **Type:** Rhythm **Genre:** Funk

These are 16th notes in three-note groups in the key of G major. Accent the first note of each group, as indicated.

WED

Workout #290 **Drum Tracks:** 22, 23 **Type:** Rhythm **Genre:** Bossa Nova

Practice these five-note groups of 16th notes; they're in the key of D♭ major.
Hint: Use the low C♯ key to play the G♯s throughout this exercise. (See Workout #258 for the fingering.)

THU

Workout #291 **Drum Tracks:** 13–15 **Type:** Rhythm **Genre:** Rock

Today's etude features 16th notes in groups of six in C# Dorian.

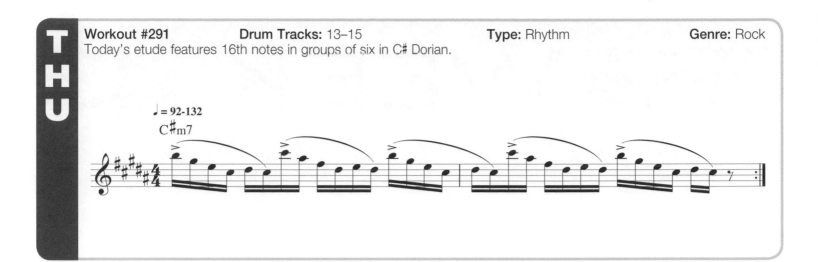

FRI

Workout #292 **Drum Tracks:** 16–18 **Type:** Rhythm **Genre:** Funk

Finally, we have 16th notes in groups of seven. This exercise is an excerpt from the Cycle of 4ths.

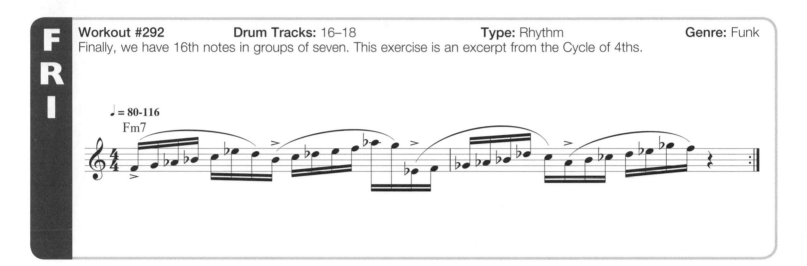

SAT

Workout #293 **Drum Tracks:** 4, 5 **Type:** Rhythm **Genre:** Swing

This exercise combines seven-note and six-note groups of 16th notes, first in G melodic minor, then F melodic minor.

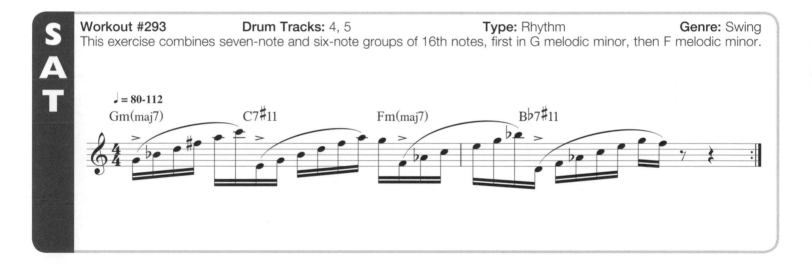

SUN

Workout #294 **Drum Tracks:** 10–12 **Type:** Rhythm **Genre:** 12/8

Have fun with this one! It's an exercise in polyrhythm in 12/8, which is conducted in 4, but may occasionally feel like it's in 3. During improvisation, it's okay to think of 12/8 in 3 or 4 as long as you can still find 1, or as one of my teachers used to say, "as long as you can pull it off."

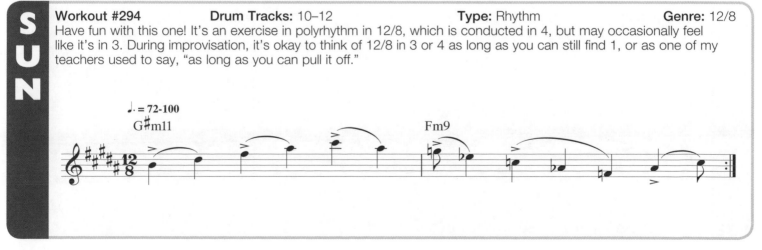

MON

Workout #295   **Drum Tracks:** 11, 12   **Type:** Rhythm   **Genre:** 12/8

Continuing our study of polyrhythms, this exercise has groups of four eighth notes over a 12/8 triplet feel.

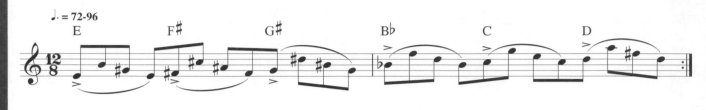

TUE

Workout #296   **Drum Tracks:** 10, 11   **Type:** Rhythm   **Genre:** 12/8

Here are some quadruplets in groups of six. The last sequence in the etude doesn't work out metrically (5 x 6 ≠ 32), so let's discontinue the sequence and get creative at that point.

Note: The example is played with the metronome on all 12 beats.

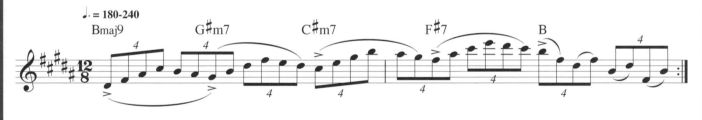

WED

Workout #297   **Drum Tracks:** 1, 2, 4, 5   **Type:** Rhythm   **Genre:** Swing

Beboppers frequently approach "goal" notes, in this case the 6th and the 9th, from a whole step above or below using chromatic passing tones. These are 16th notes in groups of three (except for the final measure (3 x 11 ≠ 32).

THU

Workout #298   **Drum Tracks:** 13, 14   **Type:** Rhythm   **Genre:** Rock

In the next three exercises, we'll attempt to demystify the elusive septuplet. Septuplets are rarely used in popular music and jazz except by a few enlightened musicians. They are difficult to decipher upon listening, and unless a player has a deep understanding of mathematics, they are probably unaware of when they are using them. Usually they are just a way to get from point A to point B in time. In this workout, septuplets are first broken into groups of four 16th notes plus a triplet followed by an actual septuplet. The divisions of the septuplet should be rhythmically even. If not, that's okay! As a colleague of mine once said, "Civilians don't know the difference."

FRI

Workout #299   **Drum Tracks:** 13, 14   **Type:** Rhythm   **Genre:** Rock

In this etude, you will need to even out your septuplets. Listen to the metronome or play-along tracks, and count eighth-note septuplets aloud for several measures before attempting this exercise. You'll need to get a feel for seven beats over two beats for this workout. This is a seven-note, 1-2-3-5-3-2-1 pattern, sequenced, and phrased in groups of two notes, similar to back-tonguing (but much more difficult).

SAT

Workout #300   **Drum Tracks:** 13, 14   **Type:** Rhythm   **Genre:** Rock

These septuplets have four-note, down-up, alternating, ascending diatonic arpeggios in D Dorian, with a surprise turnaround. I tried out several ways to phrase this exercise, and this was the easiest (ha!). Try phrasing this exercise in groups of four notes for an extreme challenge.

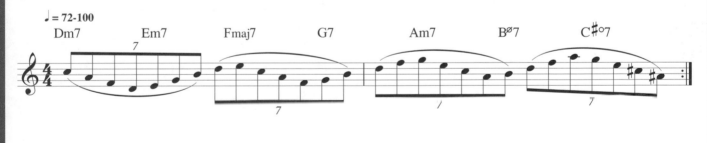

SUN

Workout #301   **Drum Tracks:** 16   **Type:** Rhythm   **Genre:** Funk

Cap off the week with this advanced rhythm workout. It should provide much-needed relief after the recent advanced polyrhythmic workouts.

MON

Workout #302 **Drum Tracks:** 13 **Type:** Technique **Genre:** Rock

There are three right-side key trill fingerings for the right hand. They are numbered starting at the bottom. In this exercise, right-side key 1 (rsk 1) is the trill fingering for A to Bb, rsk 2 is B to C, and rsk 3 is for C# to D#.

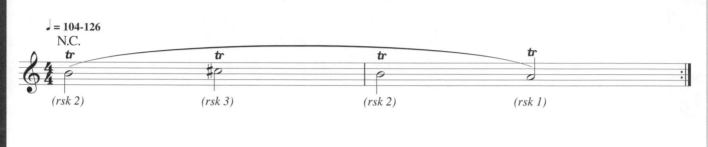

TUE

Workout #303 **Drum Tracks:** 7, 8 **Type:** Technique **Genre:** Shuffle

Here is a lick using only the right-side key 3 trill fingering to produce imperfect minor 3rds above notes in chromatic succession from high A up to C. (It would also work from B-D, especially on tenor.) This effect was used by alto saxophonist Cannonball Adderley in the 1950s and '60s, and was subsequently adopted by many rock and jazz players. Play scoops approaching the marked notes from below, but slur the whole line.

WED

Workout #304 **Drum Tracks:** 4, 5 **Type:** Technique **Genre:** Swing

Growling is an effect that has been used, and sometimes overused, by saxophonists, mostly in the rock 'n' roll genre. One could say that it was a way to simulate distortion before distortion was invented. There are a couple of different ways to do it. The least painful way is to hum (don't actually growl) an undefined drone while playing as you normally would. If you have a higher or lower voice, it will affect the sound of the growl, and everyone has a unique-sounding "growl." Try growling through this exercise, while paying close attention to all notations.

Note: The inflection in measure 2 is called a "doink." It's an upward glissando that fades out.

THU

Workout #305   **Drum Tracks:** 22–24   **Type:** Technique   **Genre:** Bossa Nova

Flutter tonguing is kind of a misnomer, because it will be impossible to tongue notes normally while executing this technique. Breath accents are the only way to articulate during flutter tonguing. To produce the flutter, roll an R, without humming, touching the tip of your tongue to the roof of your mouth away from the tip of the mouthpiece. You will probably have to use more air than usual to achieve the correct effect.

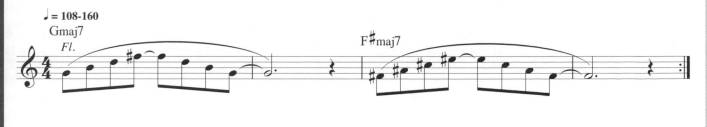

FRI

Workout #306   **Drum Tracks:** 14, 15   **Type:** Technique   **Genre:** Rock

Another advanced effect, for the elite only, is to hum the same note you are playing. Tenor saxophonist Dewey Redman used this technique as an integral part of his sound on many of his recordings. The effect is slightly garbled, sort of what it might sound like if Chewbacca played the saxophone. If this G minor pentatonic exercise seems impossible, just do the best you can. With practice, you will eventually get the feel of it. It will help if you can sing!
Note: The demo track is played on alto sax. Tenor saxes should transpose up a 4th.

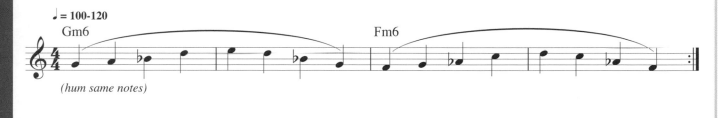

SAT

Workout #307   **Drum Tracks:** 14, 15   **Type:** Technique   **Genre:** Rock

In this admittedly difficult exercise, hum the note exactly one octave below the written note. John Coltrane was most likely the inventor of this technique. (His contemporary Pharaoh Sanders also used it.) Coltrane would often do this while playing in the altissimo range on tenor sax, which produces an astonishing screaming effect.

SUN

Workout #308   **Drum Tracks:** 4–6   **Type:** Rhythm   **Genre:** Swing

These rhythms should seem a bit confusing. Even though you may never see rhythms written this way, it is a good idea to get used to all forms of rhythmic notation.

MON

Workout #309 **Drum Tracks:** 5, 6 **Type:** Lick/Technique **Genre:** Swing

This week, let's go back and analyze some harmonic improvisation techniques. This first exercise is similar to what alto saxophonist Lee Konitz might play over this chord progression. On several key recordings, he and his counterpart on tenor sax, Warne Marsh, would often run scales and arpeggios during their solos, playing over the bar (explained in Week 8, Workout #54) with even eighth notes.

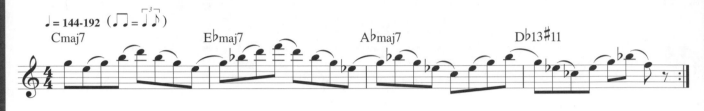

TUE

Workout #310 **Drum Tracks:** 2, 3 **Type:** Lick/Technique **Genre:** Swing

You'll love this workout. It's a fabricated example of Lee Konitz's stop-start improvisation technique, in which he would rhythmically break up oddly sequenced, anticipated arpeggios played over the bar.

WED

Workout #311 **Drum Tracks:** 28 **Type:** Technique **Genre:** New Orleans 2nd Line

Tenor sax giant Sonny Rollins utilized an improvisatory technique of weaving and winding passing tones to connect melodies using chromaticism. Hard-bop tenor saxophonist Hank Mobley was heavily influenced by Sonny's chromatic technique, which he used not only to connect his brilliant melodic ideas, but often to use the chromaticism itself as melody. This exercise is an exaggerated impression of a chromatic Hank Mobley melody.

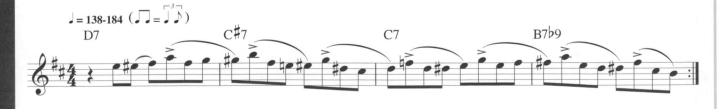

THU

Workout #312 **Drum Tracks:** 7, 8 **Type:** Lick **Genre:** Shuffle

Once in a while, the ii–V progression is modified with a built-in tritone substitution. This is an exercise in descending arpeggios with closely voiced harmony.

FRI

Workout #313 **Drum Tracks:** 19–21 **Type:** Lick/Pattern **Genre:** Jazz Waltz

This time we have lead tones in eighth-note groups of two, followed by the same lick (an octave lower) with lead tones in eighth-note triplet groups of three. The latter is similar to a lick used by trumpeter Dizzy Gillespie at a very fast tempo.

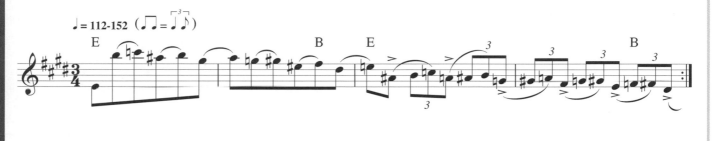

SAT

Workout #314 **Drum Tracks:** 3–5 **Type:** Pattern **Genre:** Swing

Here is a mutated version of the "Cry Me a River" lick, with altered chords resolving into Lydian dominant chords, in which the same altered lick, repeated at intervals of ascending minor 3rds, works throughout this chord progression.

SUN

Workout #315 **Drum Tracks:** 13, 14 **Type:** Rhythm **Genre:** Rock

Let's end the week with a symmetrical rhythm workout that goes up to altissimo G#. Legato tongue every note.

WEEK 46

MON

Workout #316   **Drum Tracks:** (metronome)   **Type:** Rhythm   **Genre:** Rock

This week we will have five workouts in which we'll be using the metronome only. Doing this will help you internalize time (the beat). While it is tempting to tap your foot during these exercises, don't do it, because that is externalizing time. The only purpose of the metronome is to keep time, and that is where most of your focus should be during these exercises. For Monday's exercise, set the metronome at half speed as indicated in the time signature. Imagine that the metronome is a drummer stomping the hi-hat on beats 2 and 4. It's always a good idea to start new ideas slowly; however, you may have to play faster than the suggested tempos if you have an old analog metronome, because it may not beat slowly enough.

TUE

Workout #317   **Drum Tracks:** (metronome)   **Type:** Rhythm   **Genre:** Swing

Today's B major bebop patterns are to be played with a metronome at half speed on beats 2 and 4.

WED

Workout #318   **Drum Tracks:** (metronome)   **Type:** Rhythm   **Genre:** New Orleans 2nd Line

Now for something a little more challenging: Set your metronome at one beat per measure as indicated in the time signature, and when it clicks, that will be beat 2 of each measure.
Note: On the recording, you will hear a two-measure count off.

THU

Workout #319   **Drum Tracks:** (metronome)   **Type:** Rhythm   **Genre:** Swing

An even bigger challenge, only for the bravest of souls, is to set the metronome at one beat per measure clicking on an offbeat, in this case beat 3 and a half (the "and" of 3).

Note: There is a two-measure countoff on this track, too. When you hear the click, say "and four." You will have to repeat this exercise several times before it feels even remotely natural.

FRI

Workout #320   **Drum Tracks:** 13, 14   **Type:** Rhythm   **Genre:** Bossa Nova

For this exercise, you can use the drum tracks or a metronome clicking on all four beats. This workout will help your understanding of tuplets against two beats. Try to get the divisions as equal as possible. This will take some practice.

SAT

Workout #321   **Drum Tracks:** (metronome)   **Type:** Rhythm   **Genre:** Rock

These are tuplets against four beats, which sounds easy enough, but once again we'll be setting the metronome at half speed, beating on 2 and 4 as indicated in the tempo head.

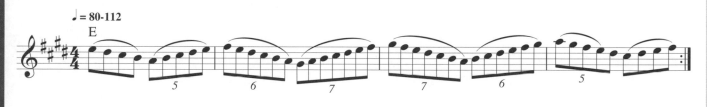

SUN

Workout #322   **Drum Tracks:** (metronome)   **Type:** Rhythm   **Genre:** Swing

Your bebop-influenced rhythm exercise for this week is in the key of Eb major. Set the metronome at half-speed, beats 2 and 4.

MON

Workout #323   **Drum Tracks:** 2, 3   **Type:** Lick   **Genre:** Swing

Turnarounds are the chord progressions that connect different sections of a composition. This week we'll take a look at some unique bebop turnarounds from the jazz repertoire. The last measure of this lick is a common turnaround used by bebop composers like Tadd Dameron and Bud Powell. There isn't much time to think about every chord change, so it's good to start building an arsenal of licks to deal with these kinds of progressions. For this exercise, ascending perfect 5ths make for a concise sequence.

TUE

Workout #324   **Drum Tracks:** 5, 6   **Type:** Lick   **Genre:** Swing

This turnaround is from the Joe Henderson composition "Isotope," in the tenor sax key. The first two measures of this exercise are all second-inversion triads following the chord changes, which are all dominant chords descending in minor 3rds. The second two measures are ascending triads in close-harmony inversions. The order of their occurrence, following the chord progression, is first-inversion D major, second-inversion B major, root-position Ab major, and first-inversion F major.

Note: The demo track is played on tenor sax.

WED

Workout #325   **Drum Tracks:** 19–21   **Type:** Lick   **Genre:** Jazz Waltz

Practice this chord progression excerpt from vibraphonist Bobby Hutcherson's "Little B's Poem," transposed for alto sax. One way to deal with chords that change on every beat is to find their common denominator. All three chords in measure 3 are derived from the A major scale, and the three chords in measure 4 are mostly derived from the D Dorian mode (C major). An ascending triplet sequence in diatonic 3rds worked well over this progression.

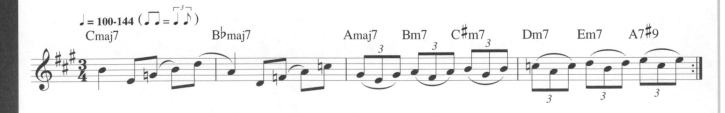

THU

Workout #326   Drum Tracks: 19–21   Type: Lick   Genre: Jazz Waltz

Joe Henderson crafted one of the most beautiful and difficult turnarounds ever. It's from his "Black Narcissus" (written in the tenor sax key). Comprised of Lydian chords, the changes are not symmetrical. One must follow the chord progression, or be lost at sea. Using short patterns works well – if you can think fast enough! For this exercise, we use the 1-#4-7 tritone pattern – in and out of sequence, depending on the chord changes – while still maintaining a melody.

Note: The demo track is played on tenor sax.

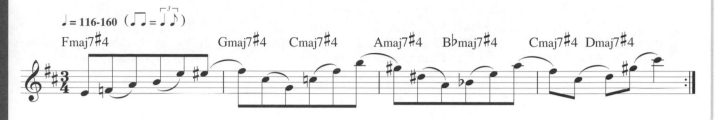

FRI

Workout #327   Drum Tracks: 4, 5   Type: Lick   Genre: Swing

The next two workouts are derived from the chord changes to Herbie Hancock's "Dolphin Dance," transposed for tenor sax. The first three measures of this, the first pedal section, are pentatonic scales and patterns following the changes: E/A, G/A, and B/A. The A dominant ♭6 chord on the last measure is the fifth mode of the D melodic minor scale, so think D melodic minor.

Note: The demo track is played on tenor sax.

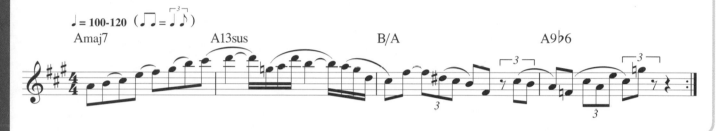

SAT

Workout #328   Drum Tracks: 4, 5   Type: Lick   Genre: Swing

These chord changes are from the third pedal section of "Dolphin Dance," which occurs just before the repeat. This workout is based on the astounding triplet-based lick that Herbie Hancock plays at the end of his first solo chorus. Take a listen to it (c. 6:47) on the album *Maiden Voyage*. In measure 1, a Cm9 arpeggio is substituted for the F9sus. Measure 2 outlines major 7th diminished chords, except the last beat and a half. What happens there is an anticipation of the chord that occurs in measure 3, a Lydian dominant chord (third degree of G melodic minor), which could also be written as a D major triad over a B♭ root. The chord on the fourth measure is an A altered chord, and the altered scale (seventh degree of B♭ melodic minor) is used.

Note: The demo track is played on tenor sax.

SUN

Workout #329   Drum Tracks: 13, 14   Type: Rhythm   Genre: Rock

End the week with this advanced rhythm and range exercise. The first three measures of this workout are different ways you will see the same rhythm written by different composers and/or copyists.

Note: The demo track is played on alto sax.

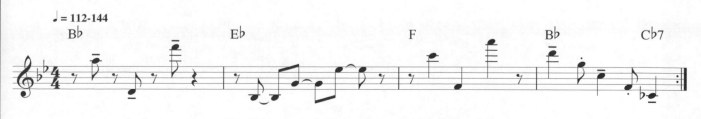

MON

Workout #330   **Drum Tracks:** 11, 12   **Type:** Rhythm/Pattern   **Genre:** 12/8

A 5-4-1 pattern played in whole steps can be used as idea-connecting material in tonal improvisation, or as melody in free improvisation.

TUE

Workout #331   **Drum Tracks:** 4–6   **Type:** Pattern   **Genre:** Swing

Today's etude is a D melodic minor arpeggio pattern, 5-3-6-4-7-5-3-1, descending diatonically in sequence (4-2-5-3-6-4-2-7, etc.).

WED

Workout #332   **Drum Tracks:** 13–15   **Type:** Pattern   **Genre:** Rock

Starting from the 3rd, the outline of an altered chord (ascending version: 3-5-8-#9) can be played over altered chords.
Note: We've seen this pattern before, in Workout #110 (Week 16). Think of this pattern as two minor 3rds, a minor 6th apart, and build from the root, third, fifth, and seventh degrees of the diminished scale.

THU

Workout #333   **Drum Tracks:** 1, 2   **Type:** Pattern   **Genre:** Swing

Here is the altered version of the melodic minor lick from Workout #331. Minor 3rds ascend in minor 2nds, jumping up a whole step to be followed by the descending version of the altered lick from Workout #332 (minor 3rds descending in minor 6ths).

FRI

Workout #334   **Drum Tracks:** 5, 6   **Type:** Pattern   **Genre:** Swing

These are major triad arpeggios (1-3-5-3) ascending in minor 3rds. This pattern works well over an altered chord, because it contains all the notes of a diminished scale. (During improvisation, you can always opt to use diminished in lieu of the altered scale.)

SAT

Workout #335   **Drum Tracks:** 14, 15   **Type:** Rhythm   **Genre:** Rock

This is another version of the previous exercise's altered/diminished lick, using first-inversion triads, first ascending, then descending.

SUN

Workout #336   **Drum Tracks:** 2, 3   **Type:** Rhythm   **Genre:** Swing

Your weekly rhythm exercise features quartal harmony following a strange chord progression. The phrasing is not written in. Make up your own phrasing. It may be slightly different than what you hear on the recorded example, and that's okay. The rules regarding modern jazz phrasing are not universal.

Notes: In jazz/swing, notes that end a phrase on an upbeat are generally played short, with a *martellato* accent (^). If you were going to sing this accent, it would sound like this: "Daht!"

SAXOPHONE AEROBICS WEEK 49

MON

Workout #337 **Drum Tracks:** 2, 3, 5, 6 **Type:** Lick/Pattern **Genre:** Swing

Within the tonality of F# Dorian, three different four-note minor 7th chord arpeggios can be outlined in their entirety: F#m7, C#m7, and G#m7.

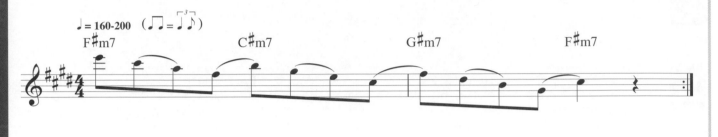

TUE

Workout #338 **Drum Tracks:** 14, 15 **Type:** Rhythm/Technique **Genre:** Rock

In this exercise, with quintuplets occurring over two beats, a 5-3-1-3-5 pattern descends chromatically to the lowest note on the horn, and back again.

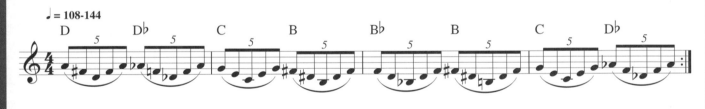

WED

Workout #339 **Drum Tracks:** 2, 3, 5, 6 **Type:** Rhythm **Genre:** Swing

Here is a similar sextuplet exercise with a chromatically ascending 3-1-3-1-7-5 pattern.

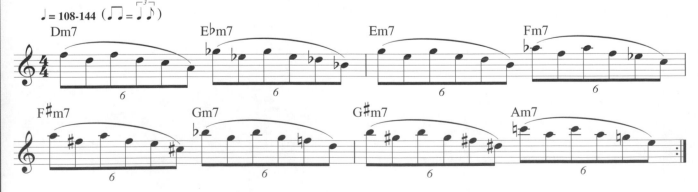

Workout #340   **Drum Tracks:** 13, 14   **Type:** Rhythm   **Genre:** Rock

And now, of course, septuplet 5-3-1-7-1-3-5 figures ascend chromatically, and return.

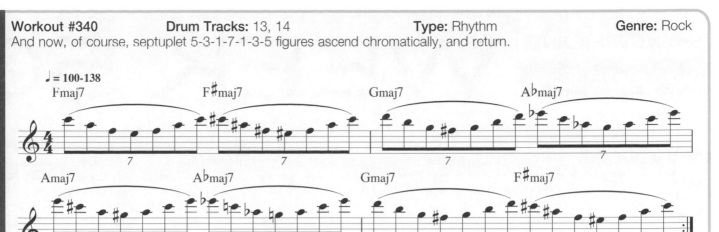

Workout #341   **Drum Tracks:** 5, 6   **Type:** Pattern   **Genre:** Swing

In this jazz etude, four-note major triad patterns (5-3-1-3) descend in major 3rds and ascend back again.

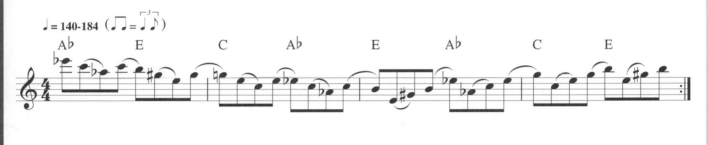

Workout #342   **Drum Tracks:** 20, 21   **Type:** Pattern   **Genre:** Jazz Waltz

Today we encounter a truncated, three-note version of the pattern from the previous exercise in 3/4 time.
Note: The phrasing is what makes this workout difficult.

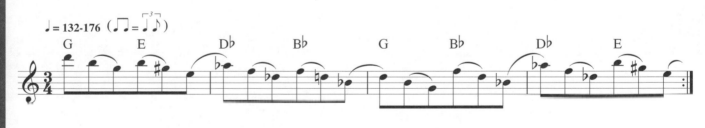

Workout #343   **Drum Tracks:** 1, 2   **Type:** Rhythm   **Genre:** Swing

Try this sight-reading rhythm workout based on some difficult etudes written by legendary sax teacher Joe Allard. However, if you find this exercise too difficult to sight read, just practice it until you can play it perfectly, with all of the implied phrasing and dynamics.

MON

Workout #344 **Drum Tracks:** 23, 24 **Type:** Rhythm **Genre:** Bossa Nova

Once again, this week we'll be working on rhythms. As you may have noticed, we haven't mentioned key signatures for a while, but we've covered all of them. It's just a fact of life as a musician that you'll be playing in all keys, especially if you ever play rock and pop music. Guitar players like to play in open-string keys like E, A, B, G, and D concert, which means lots of sharps or flats for us saxophonists. Alright, here is an exercise with odd quarter- and eighth-note combinations to further help prepare you for sight reading.

TUE

Workout #345 **Drum Tracks:** 11, 12 **Type:** Rhythm **Genre:** 12/8

Today's 12/8 workout also demonstrates some odd quarter- and eighth-note combinations. Practice it across a range of tempos.

WED

Workout #346 **Drum Tracks:** 7–9 **Type:** Rhythm **Genre:** Shuffle

When most saxophonists hear the name King Curtis (if they've heard of him), they think of the rapid-fire staccato style of playing he popularized with his solo on the Coasters' "Yakety Yak." King Curtis was one of the most influential tenor saxophonists of the 1950s, and he was a master of the triplet feel. Many of his solos have such a natural, soulful feel that their rhythmic complexity is overlooked. This exercise is similar to what he might have played over a medium shuffle.
Note: This is not a sight reading workout. Get it down as close to perfect as you can in order to hear and understand it. Many players think they already know what King Curtis was doing, but that's just because he made it sound easy.
Note: The demo track is played on tenor sax.

THU

Workout #347 Drum Tracks: 19, 20 Type: Rhythm Genre: Jazz Waltz

Have fun with these odd quarter- and eighth-note combinations in 3/4 time. End with an accent; the rest of the articulations are your call.

FRI

Workout #348 Drum Tracks: 14, 15 Type: Rhythm Genre: Rock

When sight reading a passage with a lot of same-note lines, sometimes it is easy to get confused as to where those lines are supposed to end, especially if rhythms are written in a confusing manner. Here, we have tried to make it as confusing as possible, just to exaggerate the point.

SAT

Workout #349 Drum Tracks: 29, 30 Type: Rhythm/Technique Genre: Latin

You may consider the key of A♭ major one of your least favorite keys in which to improvise. Because so few songs are written in concert B (alto) or F♯ (tenor), when one of those rare songs comes up, you're usually unprepared. It's not quite as embarrassing if you have a chance to prepare for it, and the way to do that is by practicing in all keys, every day, concentrating on the ones that give you the most trouble.

SUN

Workout #350 Drum Tracks: 1, 2 Type: Rhythm/Technique Genre: Swing

This difficult passage is based on something tenor saxophonist Bennie Wallace once played during an improvised solo. His unique style often includes an exaggeration of Sonny Rollins's technique of outlining open-harmony chords, which has not really had a sweeping influence on other players because it requires more concentration and technique than most humans possess. Nevertheless, anything is possible through practice and determination.
Note: This is not a sight-reading exercise. Take your time. The demo track is played on tenor sax.

WEEK 51

MON

Workout #351 **Drum Tracks:** 5, 6 **Type:** Pattern **Genre:** Swing

This week, we're going to work on some advanced patterns and licks that can be used for improvisation. If you want to add any of these licks/patterns to your personal repertoire, you should learn them in all keys, either chromatically or using the Cycle of 4ths. This ascending 3-♭3-1-5 pattern works well for altered (dominant #9) chords. It has great potential for modal (single-key) improvisation as well. The chord progression in the first two measures descends chromatically, and the second two measures descend in minor 3rds.

TUE

Workout #352 **Drum Tracks:** 20, 21 **Type:** Pattern **Genre:** Jazz Waltz

Here is a simple descending 5-3-2-1 pattern with a progression of ascending half steps descending in minor 3rds. It's less confusing to play it than to analyze it.

Note: For this exercise, eighth notes should be played straight.

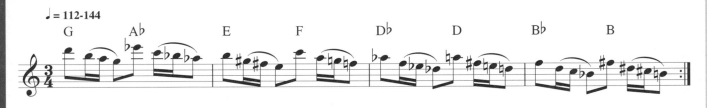

WED

Workout #353 **Drum Tracks:** 25 **Type:** Pattern **Genre:** Reggae

Work on these ascending diatonic quartal arpeggios in G major. Check the key signature; not all of the intervals within these arpeggios will be perfect 4ths.

THU

Workout #354   **Drum Tracks:** 20, 21   **Type:** Pattern **Genre:** Jazz Waltz

Today's workout is a descending version of the previous exercise with a couple of twists. First of all, note the 3/4 time signature, and secondly, instead of a consistent 7-4-1, 6-3-7 descending quartal sequence, the diatonically descending pattern is 7-1-4, 6-3-7, 5-6-2, 4-1-5, etc. As stated previously regarding some of these patterns, it's much easier to hear than to analyze.

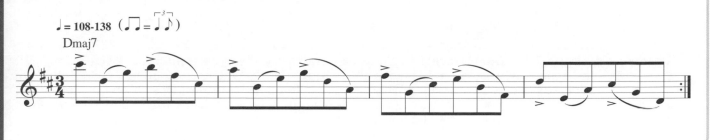

FRI

Workout #355   **Drum Tracks:** 20, 21   **Type:** Pattern   **Genre:** Jazz Waltz

This 1-2-5-7-#4-3 pattern works well for Lydian (major #4) chords.

SAT

Workout #356   **Drum Tracks:** 13   **Type:** Technique   **Genre:** Rock

The first and second measures of this workout demonstrate the Jewish Scale, or Phrygian major mode, which is the fifth degree of the harmonic minor scale. This scale is not specific to Jewish music; it is also used in Indian, Spanish, and other types of music. The third measure is also the "Jewish Scale" with downward grace notes, and the fourth measure is an ornamented descending pentatonic scale within this mode (♭7-5-4-3-1), commonly known as the Indian Pentatonic Scale.

SUN

Workout #357   **Drum Tracks:** 29, 22   **Type:** Rhythm/Technique   **Genre:** Latin

Our advanced rhythm exercise for this week is in one of the more "difficult" keys, D♭ major. (Difficult keys are tough only if you don't practice them.)

MON

Workout #358   **Drum Tracks:** 19, 20   **Type:** Technique/Scale **Genre:** Jazz Waltz

The diminished scale can be used in place of the altered scale over altered chords. If you play perfect 4ths in minor 3rds, you will have played every note in a diminished scale. In this exercise, perfect 4ths ascend in tritones, and that pattern is repeated up a minor 3rd, covering every note in a diminished scale. Measures 1 and 2 could be thought of as C°7/B, and measures 3 and 4 could be thought of as G°7/F#.

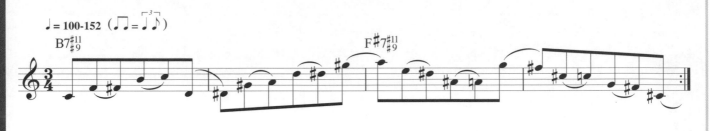

TUE

Workout #359   **Drum Tracks:** 22, 23   **Type:** Pattern   **Genre:** Bossa Nova

In this etude, we'll be practicing a D diminished scale in diatonic 3rds four different ways (up-up, down-down, up-down, down-up).

Note: The D diminished scale is also the F, A♭, and B diminished scale (as explained in Week 14, Workout #98).

WED

Workout #360   **Drum Tracks:** 16, 17   **Type:** Technique   **Genre:** Funk

Today's workout might have been included in Week 39, along with the rest of the false fingering exercises. At that point, however, it seemed to be too difficult. Since this is the last week of the book, some advanced exercises should be expected.

Note: Feel free to write the false fingering notes, which will be down a 5th or an octave and a 5th, in your book. Always use a pencil to make notes in your music. It is never, ever okay to use a pen.

Workout #361   **Drum Tracks:** 10–12   **Type:** Pattern   **Genre:** 12/8

Here is an advanced diminished five-note lick/pattern played in triplets. The five-note phrases are slurred and start with an accent. Each one of these phrases is a descending minor 3rd away from its predecessor. The odd symmetry of this lick makes it rhythmically interesting: Each phrase lands on a different beat.

Workout #362   **Drum Tracks:** 4, 5   **Type:** Pattern   **Genre:** Swing

This exercise is a popular diminished pattern among improvising musicians: Descending major 2nds in descending tritones, ascending by minor 3rds. Starting on the tonic of a C dominant ♭9 chord, every note of a D♭ diminished scale will be represented.

Note: When you see a C7♭9 chord, think D♭ diminished starting on C (as explained in Week 16, Workout #109).

Workout #363   **Drum Tracks:** 29   **Type:** Pattern   **Genre:** Latin

In this chromatic workout, measures 1–2 are descending minor 2nds ascending by minor 2nds. Measures 3–4 are ascending minor 2nds descending by minor 2nds.

Note the phrasing: Although this exercise is a study in chromatic minor 2nds, the notes that are slurred together are all a major 2nd apart, so by offsetting the whole workout by an eighth note, it becomes a study in chromatic major 2nds.

Workout #364   **Drum Tracks:** 1, 2   **Type:** Rhythm

Genre: Swing

You've arrived at the last rhythm exercise of the year, and it is advanced. The chord changes are counterintuitive and appear at random. There is also some odd notation to keep you on your toes.

DAY 365

MON

Workout #365   **Drum Tracks:** 8, 9   **Type:** Technique   **Genre:** Shuffle

For your final workout of the year, we're going to learn a new scale, the B♭ harmonic major scale. It's an uncommon scale in Western music, but a legitimate scale with its own set of modes. To play the scale in this key, it is an option to use five different trill fingerings. Use the indicated fingerings.

Note: Hold down the bis key while using the right-side key trill fingering for C.

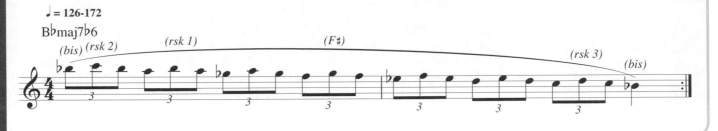

ACKNOWLEDGMENTS

I'd like to thank:

My awesome family: My wife Pam and son Jackson for putting up with me during the writing of *Saxophone Aerobics*; my parents, Dave and Bev, for supporting my talents; and the Colbo family.

My invaluable teachers: My high school band director, Jim Borgaro; my college professor, Lovell Ives; my saxophone teacher, the late Wayne Jaeckel; my late friend and mentor, Fred Sturm; Maury Laws; John Harmon; Cheryl Grosso; Trini Chavez; Terry O'Grady; Irwin Sonenfield; Steve Jordheim; Maggie Charnon; Larry Darling; Patty Darling; Ed Saxe; Jim DeKoch; and Joe Gorman.

Friends who've helped me along the way: Dane Richeson; David Cooper; Shawn Postell; Joel Arpin; Daryl Steurmer; Janet Planet; Tom Washatka; Paul Sowinski, Pat Judy, Marc Jimos, Bill Dennee, Jay Whitney, Brad Miller; Rick Piumbroeck; Matt Buchman; Nathan Behling; Steve Johnson; Andrew Lautenbach, Ken Schaphorst; Tony Wagner, Greg Koch; John and Christine Salerno; Bob Thompson; David Hazeltine; Jeff Radke at Hal Leonard; Paul Allen; Tim Pike; Randy Cooke; Andrew Doolittle; John Bohlinger; Doug Barnett; Andrew Nelson; Steve March Tormé; Danny Lueck; John Gibson; Paul Sucherman; Tim Whalen; Dave Stoler; Jeff Santaga; Darren Johnson; Alan Arber; Kostia Efimov; and Eric Hervey. I apologize if I've neglected to mention anyone who has provided me with steady work or inspiration throughout my career.

ABOUT THE AUTHOR

Suzi Johnson Hass

Forrest "Woody" Mankowski is a professional saxophonist/singer. He plays alto, tenor, and soprano saxophones, as well as flute and clarinet. He has transcribed for over 100 books for Hal Leonard Corporation and taught jazz saxophone at Lawrence University for six years.

As a studio musician, Woody has sung or played on over 500 commercial jingles for clients such as Miller Lite, Turner Classic Movies, Culvers, and Country Kitchen. He often collaborates with other musicians, including singer Steve March Tormé, guitarist Daryl Stuermer, composer Tobin Mueller, and the blues band Big Mouth and the Power Tool Horns. Mr. Mankowski is also member of [Microsoft co-founder] Paul Allen's band The Underthinkers, with whom he has performed at the Cannes Film Festival and the Super Bowl. As the male lead in *The Baseball Music Project*, Woody has appeared as a soloist with numerous major symphony orchestras, including those of Boston, Seattle, and Detroit.

Woody has backed up popular artists such as the Temptations, the Four Tops, Cheap Trick, Aretha Franklin, James Ingram, and many others. He has played in the pit orchestras for touring Broadway shows including *The Producers*, *Chicago*, and *Hairspray*.

Woody will soon be releasing an EP, his first original recording, and he will also appear as lead vocalist and saxophonist on Daryl Steurmer's upcoming album.

HAL•LEONARD SAXOPHONE PLAY-ALONG

The Saxophone Play-Along™ Series will help you play your favorite songs quickly and easily. Just follow the music, listen to the audio to hear how the saxophone should sound, and then play along using the separate backing tracks. Each song is printed twice in the book: once for alto and once for tenor saxes. The melody and lyrics are also included in the book in case you want to sing, or to simply help you follow along. The audio CD is playable on any CD player but it can also be used in your computer to adjust the recording to any tempo without changing pitch!

1. ROCK 'N' ROLL

Bony Moronie • Charlie Brown • Hand Clappin' • Honky Tonk (Parts 1 & 2) • I'm Walkin' • Lucille (You Won't Do Your Daddy's Will) • See You Later, Alligator • Shake, Rattle and Roll.
00113137 Book/CD Pack...$16.99

2. R&B

Cleo's Mood • I Got a Woman • Pick up the Pieces • Respect • Shot Gun • Soul Finger • Soul Serenade • Unchain My Heart.
00113177 Book/CD Pack...$16.99

3. CLASSIC ROCK

Baker Street • Deacon Blues • The Heart of Rock and Roll • Jazzman • Smooth Operator • Turn the Page • Who Can It Be Now? • Young Americans.
00113429 Book/CD Pack...$16.99

4. SAX CLASSICS

Boulevard of Broken Dreams • Harlem Nocturne • Night Train • Peter Gunn • The Pink Panther • St. Thomas • Tequila • Yakety Sax.
00114393 Book/CD Pack...$16.99

6. DAVE KOZ

All I See Is You • Can't Let You Go (The Sha La Song) • Emily • Honey-Dipped • Know You by Heart • Put the Top Down • Together Again • You Make Me Smile.
00118292 Book/CD Pack...$16.99

7. GROVER WASHINGTON, JR.

East River Drive • Just the Two of Us • Let It Flow • Make Me a Memory (Sad Samba) • Mr. Magic • Take Five • Take Me There • Winelight.
00118293 Book/CD Pack...$16.99

9. CHRISTMAS

The Christmas Song (Chestnuts Roasting on an Open Fire) • Christmas Time Is Here • Count Your Blessings Instead of Sheep • Do You Hear What I Hear • Have Yourself a Merry Little Christmas • The Little Drummer Boy • White Christmas • Winter Wonderland.
00148170 Book/Online Audio $16.99

HAL•LEONARD® CORPORATION

7777 W. BLUEMOUND RD. P.O. BOX 13819 MILWAUKEE, WI 53213